THE NATIONAL BALLET

Also by Arnold L. Haskell

THE SCULPTOR SPEAKS (*Heinemann*)

*

BALLETOMANIA (*Gollancz*)
DIAGHILEFF (*Gollancz*)
DANCING ROUND THE WORLD (*Gollancz*)
BALLET PANORAMA (*Batsford*)
FELICITY DANCES (*Nelson*)
PRELUDE TO BALLET (*Nelson*)
BALLET (*Pelican*)
BALLETOMANE'S SCRAPBOOK (*A. & C. Black*)
BALLETOMANE'S ALBUM (*A. & C. Black*)
BALLET—TO POLAND (*A. & C. Black*)

*

WALTZING MATILDA (*A. & C. Black*)
AUSTRALIA (*Collins*)
THE AUSTRALIANS (*A. & C. Black*)

DESIGN BY LESLIE HURRY
FOR SADLERS WELLS PRODUCTION OF *THE SWAN LAKE*

THE
NATIONAL BALLET

A History and a Manifesto

by
ARNOLD L. HASKELL

WITH AN OVERTURE BY
NINETTE DE VALOIS
AND SIXTEEN ILLUSTRATIONS

ADAM & CHARLES BLACK
4, 5 & 6 SOHO SQUARE, LONDON, W.1
1943

THIS BOOK IS PRODUCED IN COMPLETE CONFORMITY
WITH THE AUTHORISED ECONOMY STANDARD

Australia and New Zealand
THE OXFORD UNIVERSITY PRESS, MELBOURNE

Canada
THE MACMILLAN COMPANY OF CANADA, TORONTO

South Africa
THE OXFORD UNIVERSITY PRESS, CAPE TOWN

India and Burma
MACMILLAN AND COMPANY LIMITED
BOMBAY   CALCUTTA   MADRAS

MADE IN GREAT BRITAIN
PUBLISHED BY A. & C. BLACK, LIMITED, LONDON
PRINTED BY R. & R. CLARK, LIMITED, EDINBURGH

DEDICATION

*

TO

FREDERICK ASHTON

FROM A FRIEND WHO HAS FOLLOWED
HIS CREATION FROM *CAPRIOL SUITE*
TO *THE QUEST* WITH INTEREST AND
A STEADILY GROWING ADMIRATION

ACKNOWLEDGEMENTS

I AM grateful to my good friend Donald Albery and the management of the New Theatre for the opportunity of assisting at so many performances. I am also grateful to the staff of the same theatre for the unfailing courtesy and good-humour that has made the front of the house so pleasant in trying times.

I would like to thank my fellow critic Eveleigh Leith for her help in general, and Constant Lambert and Frederick Ashton for assistance in compiling the appendices, Gordon Anthony for finding me photographs at some inconvenience while on leave and Mr. G. B. L. Wilson for four admirable action photographs.

I would like to give grateful thanks to 'Anton' and *The Bystander* for permission to reproduce the admirable drawing on page 85. It shows how much classical ballet has entered into the consciousness of the British public.

My special thanks are due to Ninette de Valois, always busy on more important work, for her valuable preface, Mr. Leslie Hurry for kind permission to use his *Swan Lake* design as a frontispiece before it has been seen, and the ballet company as a whole for the great pleasure its members have given me in proving me wrong in the first place.

A. L. H.

Written at
LITTLEDEAN, GLOS.
Dec. 1942–*May* 1943

CONTENTS

vii

CONTENTS

PART II

APPENDICES AND NOTES

ILLUSTRATIONS

THE NATIONAL BALLET

OVERTURE

By Ninette de Valois

I

It would be correct to say that Arnold Haskell's present work is written for a section of the English theatre public that does not constitute *balletomania*, and is not addressed to that audience built up at Sadlers Wells Theatre before the war and known today as 'the regulars'.

Both in London and the provinces the ballet is seen these days by an increasing number of theatregoers and our new followers know little about our activities in the past.

This book is a practical guide to all our yesterdays, it gives a short account of today and expresses a viewpoint about tomorrow. It is important to emphasise that it is the work of someone who has a very practical knowledge of English Ballet from its beginnings, and who has in the last ten years of the life of the modern ballet played a unique and unusual role. He has fought great ignorance, misunderstanding and lack of interest on the part of the general theatrical public, and he has succeeded in making them regard the ballet as a very serious art of the theatre. He has also touched the general reading public. It is in this case for the general 'recognition' of ballet that we owe Arnold Haskell such a very great debt of gratitude. Also for a long time ballet was regarded as a pastime for little girls and it is one of Mr. Haskell's achievements to have opened the eyes of parents and guardians, educational institutions and the like, and convinced them that there is something in this question of ballet after all.

He has always had the English Ballet at heart—but he did one very clever thing at the commencement of its existence. He absolutely refused to become its patriotic godmother. I am afraid he did exactly the opposite. He went on praising the organisations that were flourishing abroad, until he aroused a fighting spirit in us and made us feel that we had to do something to improve our own standard and live up to that avalanche of praise which he bestowed on those foreign companies which so richly deserved it. To us he was 'Mr. Arnold Haskell' or 'that Arnold Haskell'— according to how we felt at the moment. We know now that he was genuine and sincere, and the fact that he would not praise where he did not feel it was due at the beginning was really responsible in the end for making us put our house in order.

II

All literature on the subject of current ballet tends to date extremely quickly. This is inevitable; the war makes any consistent policy hard to follow. In the following pages the author has been at pains to avoid this particular pitfall.

In the normal course of events we would have had, by now, several new periodicals in circulation devoted to the criticism of ballet. Undaunted by the present printing restriction, not a few have appeared in the form of privately circulated pamphlets or booklets. These may be termed balletic tracts—they represent the personal creeds of the earnest missionaries of the dance.

Of course these little journals are for the chosen few and their discerning disciples. Sometimes I am mildly shaken by the contents; no doubt the result of old age, and a strong feeling that I have been here and everywhere else before.

It is correct to say that I did not expect the Sadlers Wells Ballet to be in existence in the fourth year of the war; but in all fairness I must state that, in the eyes of the chosen few, it has, of course, 'expired'. It appears that it could only exist (with the true muddled thinking of balletomania) when 'they' supported it, by means of a heavy overdraft, at Sadlers Wells for two performances per week. But the overdraft and the war had no interests in common. It is as well to record that hundreds of beings, unacquainted with the auditorium of Sadlers Wells Theatre, suddenly demanded hot meals and accommodation there when the nightly blitz shattered the very foundations of Islington.

Then the Sadlers Wells Ballet indulged in unseemly and unromantic behaviour. It continued to function elsewhere; only it continued at the rate of eight and nine performances per week up and down the country, with nothing to identify it with its former existence but the name and the school.[1] It further took cover in the West End (New Theatre) and went without cover to the East End (Victoria Park).

It was then that I was presented with the first-fruits of the chosen few. Obscure and tortuous articles dealing with balletic ' commercialism' and 'decline'; explanations at great length of Balletonian Facts of Life; and the Awful Truth about Sadlers Wells. I was solemnly assured by letter, anonymous and otherwise, that 'they' stayed away from our performances. . . . Never indeed could a Viceregal Lodging in Delhi or Dublin have found life more puzzling.

. . . .

But there are bigger things and greater issues to face. Arnold Haskell has, rightly enough, dedicated this book to Frederick Ashton—and with his permission I would dedicate my chapter to the ever-increasing number of young dancers from all the English companies now serving in the Forces. Only too well do I know how much they encourage us to survive, and how well they understand how near extinction the English Ballet was four years ago.

For they know, as do their fellow artists left to keep things gay, that life today must put fact before fiction.

[1] The latter has been kept continually in existence, high up under the roof of the much-shaken Sadlers Wells Theatre.

Part I

CHAPTER I

GENERAL CONSIDERATIONS

I HAD fully determined not to write another book on ballet for the duration of the war, believing that it was worthless to waste paper on raking up nostalgic memories, while ballet marked time and confined itself to escapist entertainment rather than to recreative art in the Greek sense. But recent developments have led me to change my mind and a long indisposition has given me an opportunity to study the work in detail, after seeing no ballet for a considerable time.

At a period when our theatre seems almost bankrupt of ideas, the Sadlers Wells Ballet, now so happily in residence at the New Theatre, has shown a policy so constructive and far-sighted that it has become possible to talk of a national ballet and to visualise its position as an artistic force in the post-war international theatre world. As a medium of propaganda[1] for our national artistic ideals its importance cannot be overrated.

I shall not mention in the main body of the text the innumerable difficulties of such constructive work in war-time, but in all fairness I must touch on some of them here. There is first of all the obvious problem of man-power. At the beginning of the war some well-meaning friends of the ballet suggested that male dancers should be exempt from military service. They pointed out the excellent work the ballet was doing in maintaining morale, the injustice to dancers whose career was confined to a few early years, and the very small numbers involved. The arguments had a certain validity, but they discounted the wishes of the dancers themselves and also the terrible damage that would be caused to ballet by the sight of a group of exceptionally healthy young men standing aloof from an upheaval affecting the whole of civilisation. Those responsible for the management of the Ballet never lent

---

[1] Cardinal Richelieu was the first to use ballet in this manner. The Russians have always understood this important aspect of ballet.

4

themselves to this rather futile agitation and apart from a few dancers, not from Sadlers Wells, who suddenly found it vitally important to act as missionaries for British ballet on the American stage, the male dancer has an excellent record; all the original members of the *corps de ballet* are now in the Services.

There are other less obvious difficulties that confront a management in war-time; the impossibility of getting a supply of good ballet shoes, the difficulty of securing non-coupon materials such as tarlatan, the famine of canvas, timber and net, the paucity of electrical material and so on. As an example, the faulty lighting at times of *Les Sylphides* is due not to ignorance but to a failure in the supply of good gelatines! These are not excuses, but they might be borne in mind. I am concerned here with the direction taken by a national ballet and with the artistic and psychological problems involved, and not with accidents of a temporary and let us hope limited duration. I wish to assess the value both present and potential of a first-class achievement in our theatre.

In one sense the war has helped the establishment of a British National Ballet through the artistic isolation involved. It has hastened recognition, but the foundations were well and truly laid.

In my later writings, particularly in *Dancing Round the World*, I warned the Russian (*émigré*) companies against a policy that was leading to rapid disintegration. 1 have never concealed the fact that I believe that there is *at present* more latent talent in the average Russian company than we here possess. The average Russian dancer is more single-hearted in her devotion to the art, she does not allow early marriage to interfere with her career,[1] she is more spontaneous in the expression of her emotions. My warning lay in the gross mismanagement of that talent through commercial exploitation, a total lack of discipline in the right sense of the word, through the interminable jealousies that undermined and split every enterprise, making consistent progress impossible. I also warned those companies against their appeal to the wrong type of public, the hysterical 'fans' who took their pleasure from the technical and emotional tricks of immature personalities at the expense of creative ideas in choreography, music and scenery. Ballet had reached very much the same position as it did at the end of the Romantic movement. The next logical step led straight to the music-hall. Since

[1] The list of our talented dancers who have left the stage through marriage is a long one.

Balanchine's *Cotillon* and *Concurrence* and Massine's *Les Présages* and *Jeux d'Enfants* there was much high-class entertainment but few encouraging signs of a creative advance. I do not for a moment disparage entertainment; theatre that did not entertain would fail as surely as one that aimed at entertainment alone. Lichine, badly aided and advised, tried to call a halt and *Protée* was a small but encouraging token of that effort. Much the same was the case with the music and scenery. The post-Diaghileff Russian Ballet developed not a single composer of note and made no discoveries among decorative artists. Its most distinguished décors were by Miro and Derain. It was living on an overdraft from the previous régime. The dancing itself started full of promise with a young group led by the exceptional talent of Baronova, Toumanova, Riabouchinska and Verchinina; there were half a score of others equally worthy of development. After two seasons neither Baronova nor Toumanova had developed to any marked extent either artistically or technically. That is not to say that they did not give good and occasionally great performances, but there was no consistency in their work, which was all too often marked by irritating mannerisms. During the season of 1935 Toumanova gave a first performance of *Aurora* I have seldom seen equalled in authority and attack. Alas, it was never repeated. Baronova was more consistent, yet all too often she showed an over-awareness of the audience. Both these dancers are outstanding personalities, they have added a chapter to the history of ballet, but a small one beside the achievements of a Pavlova or Karsavina. Riabouchinska, never a ballerina but a *demi-caractère* dancer, alone continued to improve as an artist and her final London appearance in *Paganini* was also her greatest. Her dancing remained magnificently fluid, if not strong technically, and there was never an unworthy trick to enhance its effect. Her *prélude* in *Les Sylphides* sets a standard in interpretation. I suggest that she is the exception because she alone is a second-generation dancer and her mother instilled in her a respect for discipline and a strong spirit of self-criticism. Verchinina made her success in the effective combination of Central European dancing and ballet given her by Massine in *Les Présages* and was ever after cast to type. Her ideas, and she had many, were neglected in the scramble for easy and immediate success according to formula. That was the main reason for her departure from the de Basil Ballet. I have seen some of her choreographic ideas. They would greatly have enriched Russian Ballet. It remained for an American girl, Nana Gollner, to give the finest purely classical rendering of all in *The Swan Lake*, the abbreviated version.[1] Once again I must emphasise that the fault did not lie with the artists. They had exceptional talent and a whole-hearted devotion to their art. It lay with the management and with the public, among whom I by no means exempt myself, though as a close observer I may have cried halt a trifle sooner than the majority. That section of the public who 'could not live without the ballet'—it has managed to avoid the Wells for the past three years—made pets of the Russian dancers and wished them to go on doing the same thing in the same way, making no allowances for growth and character development. That charming extract *Aurora's Wedding*, instead of being an acid test of classicism, became a pretext for applauding individuals. There were exceptions, wise and critical friends—I can think of one in particular who bore on his broad shoulders the worries of the whole organisation,—but their whispers could not be heard above the din of clapping and *bravas*.

This analysis may seem ungracious from someone who has had such intense pleasure from the new Russian Ballet. It is nothing of the kind. On the contrary, it reveals a true respect for the personality of the artist. Also, it is not inserted here to try to prove that the British Ballet is in every way superior, but as an essential preliminary to the study of a national organisation. As I have already said, I believe the *average* Russian to be superior in talent and more serious in outlook to the *average* English dancer, and no one could deny the fact that the whole English structure rests on a Russian foundation. What an admirable foundation it is. I have no quarrel with those who find a certain quality in Russian dancing that is lacking in ours, so long as they do not speak from mere prejudice. In many cases they are perfectly justified; I could write at length on such a thesis. When I come to the more serious study of the dancing my conclusion will be that the company at Sadlers Wells follows the true Russian classical tradition, neglected by the Russian travelling organisations. Many of the more thoughtful Russian dancers have agreed with this diagnosis and wished for a similar chance to work in calm and harmony.

Some of the dangers that prevented the successful development of the Russian dancers are shared by our own organisation, though

[1] René Blum season, Alhambra, 1937.

with the more stolid British temperament they will be longer in revealing themselves. I shall have something to say of those dangers and of the possible means of avoiding them. Our organisation still reposes on an individual rather than on a system and it is essential to look ahead. Today's success may bear the seeds of tomorrow's failure.

I mentioned earlier on that isolation had been a good thing for the development of Sadlers Wells; a statement that needs amplification. It did not mean freedom from foreign competition; any lack of competition is definitely harmful. It meant that at an important formative period our ballet was forced to rely entirely on its own scholastic resources. It meant, also, the concentration of the public truly interested in ballet on Sadlers Wells. Many who scarcely knew that ballet existed out of the West End have been amazed at what they have missed and will certainly in the future follow the fortunes of the company with sympathetic interest.

If I do not mention other British companies, and there have been many, it is not because I am unwilling to admit that they have done or are capable of doing good work, quite apart from providing much-needed entertainment. I am interested here in continuity and development of the type shown by Sadlers Wells. I do, however, disapprove of a British company operating under a Russian disguise. The Russians have not deserved such treatment.

This question of the audience is an all-important one, quite apart from the particular economics of ballet. With the non-repertory theatre the spectator pays his money, watches, is pleased and tells his friends, or is disgusted and tells his friends; that is the end of the matter. At most he will go twice, unless, of course, he is in love with a member of the cast; such things have been known. In the case of ballet over 50 per cent of the audience come at least once a week and watch developments so closely that they feel a genuine personal interest. In the theatre the critic wields a strong influence, with ballet most of the audience are critics of some experience, if not always of the right kind. They read the critic to disagree with him, usually hysterically; my mail in the past has been ample proof of that. A change of cast provides a heated topic of discussion, and in countless ways, apart from their applause, their feelings are communicated to the management and the company. Only in ballet is an understudy thoroughly welcomed by the audience. No public performer can be totally uninfluenced by public opinion, so that a cultivated audience makes for good performances. The Maryinsky audience demanded certain technical accomplishments and were satisfied, Diaghileff's audience wished to be let into the studio secrets of the very latest artistic fads and fashions and turned on him when he gave them classicism, de Basil's audiences wanted fresh young personalities and made their stars overnight. The audience at the Wells was much the same, if the new creation did not give 'Harold' or 'June' a chance, so much the worse for the new creation. I personally was asking for one thing in particular, consistent progress, but with the halt in modern choreography and the wealth of the old repertoire the dancer interested me more than the ballet as a whole, a fault in orientation imposed by managerial policy.

While one could go on discussing various interpretations of *Les Sylphides*, it was difficult to say anything new about the ballet itself when in 1936 it was given by seven different companies in one season. That was the immediate pre-war reaction to ballet, inspired, perhaps, indirectly by the films, where the star is followed at the expense of the picture as a whole and a Ginger Rogers is wasted on the absurdities of child impersonation. What saved Sadlers Wells from being devoured by its faithful audiences was, more than anything, the fact that the classics formed such an important part of the programme. It gave both dancers and audience a sense of proportion. As a result the Wells audiences had a better balletic education than any other outside of Russia. Its 'lunatic fringe' was a clamorous one, but de Valois paid not the slightest attention to it, while visiting companies have always imagined that it had an important influence. By 'lunatic fringe', be it understood, I mean stalls as well as gallery; bank balance is not the criterion. When a prominent hostess tells a foreign manager that his programme is all wrong, he pays considerable attention. I can think of one case where the hostess in question after several seasons had not learnt to distinguish *The Swan Lake* from *Les Sylphides*, but she presumed to disapprove the performance of a certain dancer. She carried her point. That was typical of a lack of a consistent managerial policy and of settled convictions.

De Basil is a very remarkable man, possessed of boundless energy and very real courage. He not only revived a moribund art but brought it for the first time to world popularity. No one knows the full extent of his difficulties better than I do, and I doubt whether anyone else placed in a similar position could have planned more wisely. He had envisaged a permanent academy amongst other things. He was the victim of an act of disloyalty he could not have foreseen. It undermined his authority and distracted his attention. While I am concerned here with results and not with backstage history, I think it only right to correct any unjust impression that may be left by my remarks. The story of de Basil must one day be written. It will reveal to the full the debt that all ballet owes to him as well as presenting a remarkable and sympathetic personality.

CHAPTER II

PAVING THE WAY

I. BALLET IN ENGLAND

THERE is no need for our immediate purpose to trace the history of ballet in England as apart from English ballet very far back, though it would be interesting in itself. Our audiences have always been famous for their warm reception of foreign artists. 'Since I am in town', wrote La Guimard from London in 1784, 'they have not left me alone for a moment. I am overwhelmed with attentions from all the noble ladies. . . . The manner in which I am received everywhere is so flattering it might well turn a less balanced head.' Such a letter might have been written by a Baronova or Toumanova 150 years later. Théophile Gautier found London inclined to be over-enthusiastic and not sufficiently critical. Every dancer of note visited London, especially during the French Revolution. There were, of course, English dancers; one of them a pathetic figure—Clara Webster—has come down to us in old lithographs, largely on account of the fact that she was burnt to death on the stage in full view of the audience. It took an accident of that magnitude to advertise an English dancer.

After the sugary excesses of the Romantic period ballet suffered a slump everywhere in Europe save in Russia, where the serfs to whom the Russian theatre owes its vitality had kept it in contact with reality. In Paris, where it hung on at the Opéra more by habit than anything else, its greatest justifications were to serve as model for Degas and as a delight for various elderly senators who had the privilege of being seen frequenting *le foyer de la danse*. In England it found its way to the music-halls, where it maintained on the whole a far greater integrity. These lavishly spectacular ballets would not have satisfied our post-Diaghileff taste in music, décor or choreography, but the quality of the dancing was superb. That is an important point. In England we have always understood and insisted on fine dancing, in Paris the preoccupation has been with production, though in recent times the corruption of the press set all critical standards at nought and the quality and quantity of notices were paid for at a recognised rate. Apart from the 'tip', critics were given a score of seats to sell or otherwise pack the house. A full house usually meant an empty till. Finding it impossible to make ballet pay in France, de Basil made his last visit to Paris in 1934. Yet French ideas were stimulating and of value, when sifted by a true connoisseur.

In 1897 Adeline Genée, a Dane, brought up by her uncle Alexandre in the great Bournonville tradition, first cousin to the Russian, made her début at the Empire and was the outstanding figure of her time, more than two generations gaining their introduction to the art through watching this exceptionally charming and essentially intelligent dancer. Genée, an artist of dazzling technique allied with true artistry, did still more for ballet, she gave it a status and made it respectable once again after that possibly mythical but singularly unhygienic 'naughty nineties' tradition of champagne in dancers' slippers. In 1908 the Russian invasion was started by Lydia Kyasht, followed by Pavlova in 1910. A solitary English dancer, Phyllis Bedells, made a name for herself as ballerina of the Empire in 1909, but was denied the choreographic opportunities of the contemporary English dancer, her own talented daughter, for instance. She proved, however, that it could be done. Her brilliant execution will long be remembered, and she gave an active and enthusiastic collaboration to the Camargo Society, quite apart from her work in forming dancers.

II. THE ANGLO-RUSSIANS

The story of English[1] ballet begins with Pavlova and Diaghileff. No one in the modern history of dancing has had such a profound influence as Anna Pavlova; society women and suburban housewives the world over dreamed that their daughters would become second Pavlovas. I have heard of more than one case where a superstitious mother-to-be, trusting in the myth of pre-natal influence, watched *The Swan* and hoped. Pavlova, without being properly understood by the majority of her adorers—she was a far deeper artist than even they realised, and the Diaghileff public was blind to her greatness,—became a symbol of feminine grace. When the Polish and the Russian members of her ballet came to blows,

[1] I intend to use English and British in turn, each to include every race in the British Empire.

she determined to fill her company with English dancers; partly because they were more docile, but also because she genuinely admired their aptitude and the speed with which they learnt. She let them retain their English names, and the tone she maintained in the company made it as respectable for a colonel's daughter as any finishing school. That was a beginning.

Diaghileff unquestionably had a far greater influence on the art of ballet quite apart from that of dancing, but he never had the world public of Pavlova. His appeal was to a highly cultured clique and its hangers-on who finally swamped the clique. His dancers were largely drawn from the Imperial Theatres of Russia. There was, however, in his early great days, one exception—Hilda Munnings, who made her well merited fame under the name of Lydia Sokolova. Pavlova's English girls formed a well-disciplined background; Sokolova was one of the stars in a company of stars. It was the Russian Revolution that made the mass entry of English dancers into the Diaghileff Ballet possible through cutting off the supply of Russian dancers at the source.

The English girl had now before her two possibilities of dancing and 'seeing the world', with Pavlova or with Diaghileff.

And there were schools all ready to make the English 'miss' into a good Ballet-Russian. Cecchetti, the teacher of the Imperial Theatres, of Pavlova and of the Diaghileff company, formed many of them as well as a whole generation of teachers. Legat from the Imperial Theatres opened up a London studio, as did his pupil and a former Diaghileff dancer, the beautiful Seraphine Astafieva, teacher of Markova and Dolin. A number of English academies sprung up to meet the demand, varying from excellence to complete charlatanism. It is here that the Operatic Association, now the Royal Academy of Dancing, under the guidance of Adeline Genée as president and Philip Richardson as secretary, undertook the great work of supervising the teaching and of seeing through examination that it reached a certain standard of efficiency, a work that included the Dominions. There may be too many uninspired schools and too much cramming for exams, but the 'quack' is a thing of the past. All over England schools were turning out regiments of dancers, less than one per cent of whom would eventually find their way to the Russian companies. The remainder danced once a year in pantomime, became teachers in their turn or wisely settled down to a comfortable married life, richer by a little added grace and a few photographs carefully poised on the points with a pleasing toothpaste smirk. There was still a national inferiority complex, a feverish hunting through the pages of Tolstoi and Tchekov for possible and often impossible Russian names. I can think of at least two Anglo-Russians who have made themselves blatantly ridiculous.

A search through the Diaghileff programmes shows the success of the English: Sokolova, Bewicke, Savina, Coxon, Moreton, Devalois, Markova, Dolin, Doone. Pavlova's two deputy ballerinas, Butsova and French, were English, as well as such principals as the outstanding Stewart and the majority of her *corps de ballet*. As dancers the English took their place alongside the Russians and the Poles; no other nationality was represented in force. In France an English girl, Yvonne Daunt, shone at the moribund Opéra. I can think of only three French dancers[1] in any Russian company, two Danes,[2] several Slavs and only one German, who happened to be there for other reasons than that of spreading a love of art. After 1933 the Americans[3] equalled the English in numbers and aptitude.

This assumption of Russian names was in most cases perfectly legitimate. These dancers were Russian-trained, were members of a Russian company; their passports had nothing to do with the matter. Very many of them learnt Russian. They even had a tendency to overdo things. If you saw a girl in high boots dressed something like a Cossack, you could be perfectly sure that she was English. Moreover, the two nationalities understood one another remarkably well.

English dancers there were, but as yet no possibility of English ballet. Even had there been the necessary creative force, the great British public would never have permitted such presumption. They knew that dancers must be Russian, singers Italian or German, and that a good pianist's name ended in -sky, -vitch or -stein. It came as something of a shock to the public and to Diaghileff himself when an enterprising journalist published the list of Anglo-Russian dancers and managed to exaggerate the position. Diaghileff admitted the possibility of English ballet, but certainly not during his lifetime. He did not, in fact, admit the possibility of any competing company. That was his strength.

---

[1] Lebercher, Lauret, Lerina.   [2] Kirsova, Petroff.
[3] Guerard, Platoff, Gollner, etc.

The death of Diaghileff in 1929 looked at first as if it had killed ballet as a serious art. His dancers wandered about aimlessly, seeking a leader. They drifted in and out of revue. Lifar, totally unfitted for the task, found his way to the Paris Opéra and, supported by some Diaghileff hangers-on, made that moth-eaten establishment fashionable for a time. He deserves credit for that. The English dancers were thrown on their own resources, which meant Pavlova, pantomime or pedagogy; there never were so many teachers teaching others to become teachers. Now or never was the time, while the experience gained was still fresh.

It is interesting for a moment to see where the Diaghileff influence reached; in America, Fokine, Bolm, Mordkin, Semenov; in France, Lifar; in Monte Carlo (to be sent throughout the world), Massine, Balanchine, Grigorieff, Danilova; in South America, Romanoff and others; and, as we shall see, via Rambert and de Valois, through the whole British movement.

Tradition is the life-blood of ballet. Interrupt the sequence of ballet for fifteen years and you kill it. The effect would be as drastic as the burning of a library of unpublished manuscripts. *Ballet progresses by evolution and not revolution.*

Duncan, a revolutionary, had a great influence in Russia, but only through the ballet tradition. Her influence was felt in production and in choice of music and costume, but never in the classroom. Her efforts to inspire a direct revolution even during the Soviet régime were dismal failures. The Russians of all régimes realised that ballet was a scientific stage training, a means and not an end, that the ballet-trained dancer could perform *à la* Duncan but that a Duncan was severely limited by her self-imposed technique. We in this country have shared the Russian respect for tradition, and Central Europeanism has had not the slightest effect here. We know that if our dancers can perform *The Swan Lake*, they can perform any other work, barefoot or on points—result, *Dante Sonata.*

These are points to be remembered before reading the next chapter. Its title, 'Towards a National Ballet', might be paraphrased, 'towards the planting of a continuity of tradition'.

CHAPTER III

TOWARDS A NATIONAL BALLET

I. BALLET IN DANGER

THE problem in ballet has never been the supply of dancers, and this was specially so in the case of England where girls of all shapes and sizes found their way to the dancing schools. The need has always been to find a strong directing force possessed of a knowledge of the component arts and of absolute artistic integrity. There are twenty *potential* Nijinskys for one Diaghileff. Where there are state-subsidised institutions with a strong tradition the position is different, and in the interim between good directors the ballet can mark time without running the risk of disintegration. Vsevolojsky gave the Imperial Ballet new life, Teliakovsky lowered its reputation, but it continued unshakable.

Economically speaking, the Diaghileff Ballet was never a sound proposition and relied entirely on the subsidies of its wealthy patrons. With his great prestige that was possible in spite of many close shaves and a major disaster in 1921 with *The Sleeping Princess*. No one else could hope to follow on those lines. It became a fixed belief that ballet was an art for the wealthy that could not possibly pay, though Pavlova had proved conclusively to the contrary. This wish to run things *à la* Diaghileff without his individual touch (I use the word in both its senses) was a considerable handicap to any enterprise. It is one of the main reasons for the decadence of Russian post-Diaghileff ballet. The waste of money through faulty planning was appalling, and if a patron did put up the money, he attached conditions that had little to do with art.

Three groups of people, working independently and at the same time co-operating in a spirit that is only possible with the much-abused British temperament, formed the beginnings of British ballet proper, largely on overdrafts and promises and totally without the support of those wealthy patrons who professed to love the ballet. It should be placed on record that the Wells, the Camargo, the Ballet Club were started and run by professionals and, on the other side of the footlights, by the general public; they owed nothing to any Maecenas.

The first spectacular effort was that of the Camargo Society, founded in 1930 by P. J. S. Richardson and the present writer. The Camargo was a management without a company, a shop-window without a store, so that first it is necessary to study the groups that it used.

II. MARIE RAMBERT

Marie Rambert had been a pupil of Jacques Dalcroze and was chosen by Diaghileff to teach the principles of eurythmics to the Russians. She soon became an enthusiastic convert to classicism and a pupil of Cecchetti. She started a London studio and there formed a group of pupils, brought up on the classics. Her method differed from that of the majority of teachers in that she made the ballet-stage the goal of her teaching, concentrating on the development of stagecraft and personality. Her pupils were no doubt destined for the Diaghileff Ballet, but when he died she kept her little group intact and its members were animated by the spirit of a company.

Marie Rambert was the first by her teaching to put the English girl on a level with the Russians, psychologically speaking. She broke down the reserve and the old school principle of not shining if it were possible to remain hidden in the team. She stung her girls into becoming *solistes* and they showed countless others that it could be done. She has done great things, but that especially must be remembered. One saw a plump schoolgirl enter her studio doors; a term later she came out as an attractive personality. Rambert's 'babies' held the stage many years before de Basil's and before the Wells had revealed any personalities.

As early on as 1930 she gave a highly successful matinée at the Lyric, Hammersmith, that was far more creative than any pupil show. Among those young dancers were some who were destined to play a major role in our story, all were pioneers—Pearl Argyle, Diana Gould, Prudence Hyman, Andrée Howard, Maud Lloyd, Elizabeth Schooling, Frederick Ashton, Harold Turner and William Chappell; all of them dancing under the then serious handicap of English names. Later, Karsavina and Woizikovsky paid these young dancers the unique compliment of appearing with them for a season.

Let me recall some of their achievements too easily forgotten: Prudence Hyman in *Bluebird*, technically not strong by later standards but with an appearance of *brio* and holding the stage. It was an unheard-of thing for so young a dancer to dare the role; the same artiste as Columbine in *Carnaval*, a really memorable interpretation; Diana Gould, looking like a Giorgione, as Leda in Ashton's ballet or in the Pavane from *Capriol Suite*; the charming subtle artistry of Andrée Howard in *The Florentine Picture*; and later Maud Lloyd in moments of *The Swan Lake* in which she attained real beauty; and finally Pearl Argyle in everything she did, but most of all in *The Lady of Shalott*, where for the first time a feeling of drama broke through her beautiful serenity— but more of her later.

These achievements belong to the history of our ballet, and I am happy to remember that I had a very small hand in the work and was a member of the audience in the days when it was painfully scanty; fourteen in front one memorable night, and some of those hospital nurses! Later this company was rewarded by an international reputation.

Before dealing at length with Frederick Ashton, mention must be made of Pearl Argyle. One of the main handicaps under which the native dancer suffered was an alleged lack of glamour. Sokolova had it in plenty (Munnings was kept a secret for many years), and in any case the word has no positive meaning. Would Melba have succeeded as Nellie Armstrong? Pearl Argyle was never an outstanding technical dancer, but she was a mature personality, a true artist and the greatest beauty to appear on the modern ballet stage. So highly did I value that mature personality that I compromised myself seriously through praising a performance in which Pearl Argyle was technically inadequate. My critics were doubtless justified, they were not mind readers; but the manner in which Argyle stepped out onto the stage and confronted the audience, in a style I had not seen before in an English, apart from an Anglo-Russian dancer, made nothing else of any importance that night. I might have expressed myself better, though the space was restricted, but on mature reflection I would have done the same again. When I was tired of the classroom, Pearl Argyle gave me theatre. To the historian apart from the critic her role, brief as it was, cannot be over-estimated. She created for herself a public that might not otherwise have watched the inspirations of an Ashton, however promising these were. She attracted the attention of Balanchine and appeared in his *Ballets 1933*. She deserves an honoured position as a pioneer of British Ballet, far more so than the Anglo-Russians, always a little unhappy in their new surroundings and bringing with them their personal public.

All these efforts would have come to nothing without a choreographer. Diaghileff himself had suffered through the lack of choreography, and after the dismal failure of Lifar with *Le Renard* his position would have become acute.

Frederick Ashton came to ballet comparatively late, after a conventional public school education. He became at first a casual pupil of Massine's and then went to Marie Rambert. She soon saw his remarkable creative talent and gave him the opportunity to develop and to experiment. An association with Nijinska, through the temporary Ida Rubinstein company, proved a valuable lesson in how the choreographer handles a large company. Ashton's first important work, *Capriol Suite*, mounted on the small Rambert company, proved more than promising and attracted immediate notice, earning the interest of Pavlova. She had offered him a contract shortly before her death. Other works, such as *Leda*, showed that *Capriol Suite* was not merely a lucky chance. Those ballets and *Florentine Picture*, Ashton's juvenilia, belong to our ballet history. I would like to see a properly kept archive. It will soon be too late to preserve a memory of all these works.

Also from her studio Rambert developed the decorative talent of William Chappell. She gave Sophie Fedorovitch and Nadia Benois their first decorative opportunities. She had a miniature and self-contained ballet company.

III. MARKOVA AND DOLIN

The next group to assist were the Anglo-Russians, Markova and Dolin. Both had been trained in the London studio of Seraphine Astafieva and had joined the Diaghileff Ballet. Dolin had made a brief but spectacular success; Markova had shown rare promise,[1] but the company had been disbanded before this could come to fulfilment. They had made various pantomime and music-hall appearances, but Markova, an artist of high integrity, had never been at home in such an atmosphere and it remained for Ashton

[1] 'Watch my little English girl.'—Diaghileff.

to launch her on her second great career, building for her a number of dazzling roles in which her virtuosity could find full play. She in her turn developed Ashton's gifts and drew attention to his skill. Dolin lent his prestige and his fine aptitude as a partner, though he was always too much of an individualist to become closely identified with the movement.

IV. NINETTE DE VALOIS

The third and the most important force in the founding of the National Ballet was Ninette de Valois, *née* Edris Stannus. I have written of her at considerable length elsewhere in a book dedicated to her[1] and I will do no more here than to summarise. The National Ballet is largely her creation and rests on her today. One day I shall be tempted to write a whole book on this important and fascinating subject. She started as something of a child prodigy and fortunately survived much fulsome praise, including a cutting I have by me, 'this child is a poem'. After a number of such engagements as were then available to the talented dancer she joined the Diaghileff company in 1924 as a small *soliste*, her finest work being in the 'finger' variation from *Aurora's Wedding*; but everything she did was conspicuous for its neatness of execution and the obvious intelligence behind it.

Two years later she left a company that was the ideal of every dancer almost all over the world, apparently dissatisfied with the direction the ballet was taking during what we can now see was undoubtedly Diaghileff's weakest period. As the majority of dancers judge ballet, not unnaturally, by the number and importance of their roles, and as de Valois was admirably treated by Diaghileff in that respect, her decision was amazing. More so still when she settled down to found a school with a programme to which she gave the ambitious name of Academy of Choreographic Art. In those days she was earnest, apparently self-confident yet very eager to seek offence. The writer has been the recipient of more than one angry letter; deserved no doubt. She turned her back on the frivolous in ballet, the terribly 'amusing' creations of the 20's. So frightened was she of any suggestion of flippancy that she was in grave danger of becoming a bore, and her most noteworthy production, *Rout*, did not seem to justify

[1] *Ballet* (Pelican books).

her decision. Yet the Academy of Choreographic Art can lay claim to greatness; it produced one outstanding choreographer, Ninette de Valois, and a group of dancers, among them Ursula Moreton, pioneers of her new movement. With the Academy as her headquarters she travelled to the Abbey Theatre, Dublin, and the Festival Theatre, Cambridge, where she worked with actors untrained in ballet proper. Much of her work there anticipated what St. Denis showed us in his remarkable *Théâtre des Quinze*.[1] This started by giving her an unusual knowledge of the stage and the relationship between dancing and theatre. It made her into a producer, which is something quite apart from the functions of choreographer; an alliance of the two leads to a *Petrouchka* or *Rake's Progress*. It also gave her a certain poise. She had begun to justify her decision through creation, she was meeting people who appreciated her quality and she was no longer in the aggressive mood of the thwarted creator. I have laughed at the Academy of Choreographic Art; I was wrong. Today I must give it its lawful place in the scaffolding of the National Ballet. When the Camargo Society created the demand it was ready to take its place and the Camargo became the shop-window for the Rambert and de Valois groups.

V. THE CAMARGO SOCIETY

The Camargo Society was, as I have said, a management without a company. It had no clearly defined aesthetic policy, and wisely so; its aim was to develop and encourage the talent available; an aesthetic policy would emerge as soon as a personality was developed to take over from the committee. No committee can run an artistic enterprise. It was strongest in its musical direction under the guidance of the experienced Edwin Evans with his vast knowledge and catholic taste, and Constant Lambert, who was to become a pillar of the National Ballet. It owed a great deal to one Russian dancer, Lydia Lopokova, who not only lent her artistry and great prestige but her unswerving faith in its value at a time

[1] His whole system of theatrical education insisted on a knowledge of movement in the actor and choreography in the producer, as those who remember *La Loire* and *Lucrèce*, the finest of all pre-war productions, will realise. I would like to see the position reversed and a knowledge of drama indispensable in the dancer's education, and by drama I do not mean conventional mime. Fokine's rehearsals were true lessons in acting. He alone among choreographers consciously developed this all-important aspect.

when it was fashionable to believe that the ballet was buried with Diaghileff in Venice. Her husband, then Mr. J. M. Keynes, not only managed the difficult finances of the company, but showed an equal faith, understanding and knowledge. Without them the Camargo might easily have collapsed and with it all hopes of future English creation.

I will not deal with the endless difficulties that confronted the committee and its energetic secretary, Mr Montagu-Nathan, such recitals are monotonous, but I must mention that all the artists concerned gave their services eagerly and so made the enterprise possible. When we study the repertoire we can see that the results were impressive. For generations English dancers had been awaiting just such a chance; when it came they seized it. Frederick Ashton, at that date by far the most mature, revived the already popular *Capriol Suite* and created *Pomona*, *My Lord of Burleigh*, *Rio Grande* and *Façade*. Ashton possessed to a high degree—he has advanced far beyond that point—the gift of fitting a role to an individual. Constant Lambert's *Pomona*, a ballet in the direct Diaghileff idiom, composed around the very feminine personality of the Chicago dancer Anna Ludmilla, was an immediate success. The public had expected to patronise a glorified pupil show and they found something highly sophisticated, something with style and finish. This ballet has been revived at Sadlers Wells with both Pearl Argyle and Margot Fonteyn and will bear further revival. *Capriol Suite* made both Ashton's and England's creative possibilities obvious to the connoisseur, *Pomona* showed them to the general public. It was a landmark. *My Lord of Burleigh* was a charming *suite de danses* to music by Mendelssohn, skilfully wedded to a Tennyson libretto by Edwin Evans. It is a work of great charm and exploits English romanticism as *Carnaval* did German of the Biedermeier period. I would willingly see it again, a true dancer's ballet. Lambert's *Rio Grande* with a décor and costumes by Edward Burra was in the later Diaghileff tradition, a work that dated when I saw it revived in 1936, but that had a certain quality and roles in which Lydia Lopokova and Alicia Markova excelled. *High Yellow* done in collaboration with Buddy Bradley was a balletic exploitation of negro tap in which neither medium was really at home. In spite of Fred Astaire's great artistry, tap belongs to the negro and only has a meaning when tapped by the feet of a Robinson or other great coloured performers. It can never give anything to ballet; yet it was fair entertainment. In *Façade*, which, considerably amplified, has never left the repertoire, there was much riotous fun and more besides. It is so amusing that one might easily lose sight of the extraordinary skill with which it was composed, the wit as well as the humour of the dancer poking his fun at every type of dance and dancer. And it was an entirely new departure in ballet, a true creation in no known style. Ashton immediately captured a large section of the sophisticated public. Lopokova and Markova created two of the most striking roles, the milkmaid and the polka dancer, but over a dozen dancers have since proved the worth of the choreography. In future programmes this was to be the ideal tail-piece.

Ninette de Valois proved herself in an entirely different direction with the creation of an intensely serious work, *Job*, based on the drawings of Blake with music by Vaughan Williams. This majestic work, produced in the grand-manner-simple, compelled a somewhat grudging admiration. It was not immediately recognised as ballet by those who were used to the Diaghileff formula, or to the use of the adjective 'amusing' as the limit of their praise, though had they understood the true meaning of Fokine's and Noverre's dicta they would not have allowed a play on words to mar their pleasure. It was not only ballet but the type of ballet after which many earnest experimenters in Central Europe and the United States had been groping, a true dance-drama.[1] It was also the very first sign of a national outlook.

It has always been easy, a true trap for the superficial, to take some painter and make groups from his pictures that will gain instant recognition. 'Look, dear, that's the picture in the National Gallery. How very clever; one, two, three, four, five, six angels —they're all there.' It had been done for years with groups from Greek vases; later de Valois, in one of her few artistic failures, did it herself with Manet's *Bar aux Folies Bergère* and gave us a mixture in which Lautrec predominated, not unnaturally, since it was impossible from the beginning to make a ballet out of the purely plastic Manet. In *Job* she created a thousand pictures each one of which bore the unmistakable stamp of Blake. Later she repeated this *tour de force* with Hogarth and Rowlandson. In the less

[1] This word 'dance-drama', which German writers have described at such tedious length, is nothing new. Noverre wrote of it and put it into practice, Fokine has done so in our day.

popular *Création du Monde* she tackled a problem that had defeated the Swedish Ballet of Jan Borlin with a rare musical skill, weaving intricate patterns as her world was born. I would like to see a revival of this. I remember Edward Wolfe's décor as a particularly distinguished piece of work. Ashton had already proved himself to many, here was a new choreographer who had sprung up, fully mature, at a moment when she was most needed. Her two works in a lighter vein, *Cephalus and Procris* and *The Origin of Design*, were worthy, earnest and a trifle tedious. They were characterised, however, by that superb craftsmanship that never deserts her. The ideal programme needed both Ashton and de Valois.

Two years after its formation, the Society was able to sponsor a month's season at the Savoy Theatre with Spessiva, Lopokova, Markova, Dolin and the dancers who had appeared at the special performances.

This was the true beginning.

The critics were extraordinarily kind to the new venture; had they been otherwise they might have killed it at birth. One of them, C. B. Mortlock in the *Daily Telegraph*, saw the historic importance of the occasion, as he had done in the case of the first Camargo performance, and stressed that point of view. Also, it was the only ballet to be seen in London, and London had a large public for ballet. Diaghileff was dead, followed by Pavlova two years later. The atmosphere was one of gratitude. It remained to be seen whether these groups could remain together in harmony and create enough to satisfy their public.

Summing up English choreography at this time, I wrote: 'Obviously our choreography today is still immature, as is most of our dancing, and it is quite impossible to judge it from the same critical standards as we adopt for the Russians. We have no choreographers sufficiently inspired themselves to inspire a company or with sufficient authority to discipline them perfectly. Most important of all, they have not yet a full knowledge of the possibilities of movement, either physical or academic, so that the vocabulary in use is an extremely limited one, and the performance of any work is apt to depend on one brilliant dancer alone.'

This struck a harsh note in the general chorus of praise, but it was true. There was nothing immature about *Job*, but *Job* was and remains an exceptional work outside the development of choreography. In *Pomona* Ashton was only beginning to devise movement for a *corps de ballet*, and the actual *enchaînements* used by de Valois in her other works were strictly limited. Adrian Stokes, still more outspoken, talked of 'bird-like twitchings' and a 'vulgarisation of the puppet side of ballet'. He was clearly wrong. English choreography suffered from only one defect, that of immaturity. It was always on the right lines. The English choreographer working with the experienced ballerina was at a disadvantage. When he could work for a dancer he had played his share in creating both could develop. Within a comparatively short period the whole vocabulary of movement had extended. My harsh criticism of yesterday would be admitted by the most fervent Wells supporter today.

Whether I believed in the possibility of such a development is another matter.

In presenting *Pomona*, *Façade*, *Job* and revivals of the abbreviated *Swan Lake* and *Giselle*, the Camargo Society had fulfilled itself. All considerations of finance apart, there was nothing more that it could do.

Between the first and second performances Marie Rambert, who had already been a pioneer with her company, created the Ballet Club to give it a permanent headquarters, and with it a new medium, 'chamber ballet'. Ashton developed, new choreographers came to the fore in Andrée Howard and Anthony Tudor, and the Rambert dancers gained valuable experience. These miniature productions had an elegance and a finish that surpassed anything to be shown by English ballet for some time to come. The small stage made attention to detail essential; but, after a time, it hampered full expansion, confining the company to the medium of 'chamber ballet'. In this way Marie Rambert lost many of her 'discoveries', without however losing their gratitude or that of the public. Both her work and the necessity for it continues.

In the same interval between the first and second performances of the Camargo Society the Sadlers Wells Ballet was formed, attracting comparatively little attention.

VI. CREATION OF SADLERS WELLS

In 1931 that remarkable woman Lilian Baylis, who had without the financial means accomplished what was done by the state in other countries,[1] added Sadlers Wells to her responsibilities at the

[1] Old Vic and Sadlers Wells = Opéra, Opéra Comique, Odéon, Théâtre Français.

Old Vic. She trusted in the Almighty with a simple and steadfast faith to meet the continual difficulties that arose. She worked as well as prayed and her motto was always 'if you want something done, whether you can pay his price or not, always ask the best person for the job; never make a compromise. The big people understand and are ready to help.' So she asked Ninette de Valois to form a small ballet company to dance in the Vic-Wells operas. Baylis was no connoisseur of art, but she understood human nature as few have done, and once she gave her trust to anyone she was prepared to give him a free hand—as far as finances allowed—and to back him to the limit. If she did not see where her offer would lead, de Valois did. It involved a considerable sacrifice to abandon a prosperous school and various theatrical undertakings and to launch a ballet company consisting of eight girls. In spite of the Camargo successes it meant starting at the very beginning; the ballets in *Faust* and *Carmen* offer little scope and attract no attention unless they are comically inadequate. De Valois realised that with a theatre school under her control she could arrive at something permanent. She started with the opera ballets, then with an odd evening devoted entirely to ballet; next the company was enlarged, guest artistes appeared and with no flourish of trumpets the National Ballet was born, inheriting much of the Camargo repertoire and a small but useful sum of money that remained over after J. M. Keynes' skilful handling of the funds.

In 1933 the London public that had been forced to rely on English talent for the past four years was treated to a regular Russian Ballet Festival. Edward James started by presenting a short and expensive season at the Savoy with the fourteen-year-old Toumanova, Tilly Losch, Lifar, Nikitina and Doubrovska, followed by the memorable five-months season of the de Basil company at the Alhambra. The focus was immediately altered. *Les Ballets 1933* did not find success; de Basil became a London institution and his young company set entirely new standards of execution. The years of *balletomania* had started. I have dealt with that period elsewhere; it only concerns us here through its effect on the small company struggling for recognition at Sadlers Wells. That effect might have been disastrous; on the contrary it was highly beneficial. It set a very high standard of dancing and production, it killed the cloying atmosphere of adulation that always surrounds an enterprise just out of the pupil stage, and it aroused all the native aggressiveness in de Valois. When you do that, a positive reaction is inevitable. Instead of being discouraged she saw the value of her own company's work, and if at this distance one compares the giant at the Alhambra and Covent Garden with the dwarf at Sadlers Wells, the result is highly interesting, and gets down to the very bedrock of my argument. De Basil had at his disposal more talent than he was able to use, both mature and immature: Danilova and Baronova, Massine and Lichine. He had the prestige of Diaghileff's mantle and, more important still, the entire Diaghileff repertoire from Fokine to Balanchine, some thirty works that were proven successes.

What was not immediately apparent, after the loss of Monte Carlo, he had no permanent home, no school apart from the morning class, and his success kept him on numberless exhausting journeys during which it was impossible to create. Those American tours with their one-night stands and the temptations of Hollywood and 'musicals' caused more damage than the inability to create. Think of it, 103 towns in six months and the company was proud of its record in mileage! The performances that I saw in the smaller of those towns would have been hissed off the stage over here. Native American ballet, the Ballet Caravan and the Philadelphia Ballet were doing sounder work without the success, for the identical reasons already mentioned.

Sadlers Wells had one popular ballerina, Markova, with a public of her own and a background, very markedly a background, of well-trained dancers. They had a small repertoire with nothing to fall back upon, and no prestige whatsoever. Their assets were a permanent home, a ballet school, freedom from overwork, Ninette de Valois, Frederick Ashton and Constant Lambert, also the necessity of discovering and using all the talent at their disposal. This last is a question that interests me particularly.

I could quote many examples of wasted talent, but one is particularly striking as it reveals much that was wrong with the 'giant' at the Alhambra, but not apparent at the time.

De Basil engaged a fourteen-year-old English girl from a famous Paris studio. She was unusually beautiful and definitely talented. Everyone was agreed about her talent. She went to America a number of times, to Australia twice and by then she was nineteen. Everyone was still agreed about her talent and the necessity of doing something about it. But there was no time. L. could not even console herself that her chance would come when she was a little older, for the ballerinas were all the same age, she could not say to herself that one day she would be noticed; she was noticed from the start, only there was never any time to teach her anything. From her point of view the story has a happy ending, she married; but such waste of talent, for such a reason, could not have happened either with Diaghileff or at the Wells. And all the time those who had fallen into leading roles were being burnt out through overwork.

VII. A CONSTRUCTIVE POLICY

It is in the building of the repertoire that the Wells showed their initial skill. Markova, a purely classical ballerina, was their trump card. She made possible a series of classical revivals—*The Swan Lake* in its entirety, *Casse-Noisette*, *Giselle*, while *Coppélia* was revived for Lopokova and de Valois. These revivals did far more than fill the repertoire; they trained a whole generation of dancers in the old Russian manner, impossible with the new ambulant Russians. The classics are the syntax of ballet. Dance the classics well and everything is possible. As the home of the classics Sadlers Wells had not only a new prestige, but had given itself a tradition in the only possible way.

The new repertoire built up by de Valois and Ashton was a success, and success in ballet means the production of works that find a permanent place in the programme; first-night applause is not sufficient. I will name some of the productions here and leave them for discussion later. De Valois—*The Rake's Progress*, *Checkmate*, *The Gods Go A-Begging*; Ashton—*Les Rendezvous*, *Les Patineurs*, *Wedding Bouquet*, *Apparitions*, *Le Baiser de la Fée*, *Nocturne*.

What immediately distinguished the new company was its use of music. The Russians had little time to give to musical thought. Diaghileff with headquarters at Monte Carlo had gathered around him a coterie of distinguished musicians. The de Basil conductors had little else to do but to rehearse, conduct, pack evening suits and band parts, with an occasional dispute with some orchestral union by way of diversion. The policy of the Russian Ballet was to use any classical music that came to hand, with uneven choreographic results. Had de Basil and Blum remained together they might have complemented one another and the material could have been prepared at Monte Carlo. Blum was a man of consider-

able taste. I have never sympathised with those critics who con-
demned the use of classical music for dancing. They should
remember that ballet is more closely related to the theatre than the
concert-hall. But the selection and arrangement of already composed music requires a very high degree of skill and judgment, as
Diaghileff showed in the case of *Les Sylphides*, *The Good-humoured
Ladies* and *Schéhérazade*. The use of symphonic music may succeed
in certain cases, it may succeed in portions. The whole thing is a
question of sustaining the choreographic interest and keeping it on
a parallel with the composer's thought. Time is the essence of the
matter. A musical theme may be sustained for over ten minutes,
the ballerina cannot manage more than three, the music may allow
for a lift and then keep the dancer in the air and so on. *Choreartium*
(Brahms' 4th Symphony), in parts a really great choreographic
work, is full of such examples. The symphonic ballet could never
become a fixed policy and the success of *Les Présages* and the partial
success of *Choreartium* were bound to give way to the utter failure
of Beethoven's 7th Symphony, rightly called the apotheosis of
the dance, for the very reason that it required no danced interpretation.

While the Russians marked time musically, Lambert laid down
for the Wells a policy of musical integrity that greatly enhanced its
reputation. The music for *Les Patineurs*, *Les Rendezvous* and *Apparitions*, for instance, was as happily chosen as any of Diaghileff's
selections and the scores remain valid musical suites without the
dancing that summoned them into being. In the case of music by
contemporary composers the record stands equally high with Lambert, Walton, Bliss, Berners, Vaughan Williams, Gavin Gordon.
That is at the back of the successful foundation of Sadlers Wells;
*a strong classical repertoire, and choreography based on a true musical
policy*. Those factors alone maintained the company in the beginning. Its home and its school gave it growth.

In December 1935 Markova left with Anton Dolin to form her
own company. The fortunes of that company do not concern
us here, though they show the impossibility of building on individuals however good. Markova was a brilliant individual and it
might have seemed to the superficial that the Wells had been built
on her, its solitary star. Certainly her particular gifts had suggested
and made possible the classical repertoire. I have noticed that it is
an infallible rule that in the long run the classics provide their own

dancers; note the many *adequate* Blue Birds the Wells has found.[1] It needed courage to part with Markova and not to replace her by another dancer of note. I can remember at the time believing in the company sufficiently to applaud de Valois in her resolve. The school had been in existence long enough to form a group of dancers. In a really good company no dancer is indispensable, that is one of the standards of a good company; and so it proved.

Let us here pay tribute to Markova. She set the Wells a fine example, she helped to build its public. She herself grew with the opportunities it afforded her. It was natural that she never really formed a part of the company. It was Markova *and* the Sadlers Wells Ballet, artistically always an unsatisfactory combination, and while she remained no one else could shine, not because of her character or personality, but because it had started so. She returned to where she really belonged, as the bright ornament of a Russian Ballet. When she left, the company could start life as a personality on its own. That is the characteristic of every great company, something more than a collection of stars. The greatest of all, the Diaghileff company, was more important than any of its individuals. When Nijinsky left, he and others thought it would mean the end of Diaghileff. Instead it meant the end of Nijinsky, making no real difference to the company. Massine stepped into his place with an even greater success. When Massine left, he did little good while away, but the Ballet flourished with Woizikovsky in his place, a lesser artist but a better dancer. The Pavlova company could not exist without Pavlova; it never acquired a personality of its own.

That is a point that needs driving home to ballet-lovers. The individual dancer is important for a few seasons. If she is that rarity, a great ballerina, she will not readily be replaced, but, if the company is a living thing, replaced she will be, and the admirers of the new ballerina will be applauding her with equal fervour. 'La reine est morte, vive la reine.' That is a motto for dancers and their admirers. The company alone counts.

What is this company that we can and should talk of as a living thing? It is a school, a theatre, a musical director, a manager, a stage-manager, a series of choreographers; it is the record they

[1] I watched Pamela May, the finest Blue Bird—her performance was far more than adequate—grow up in the Wells atmosphere into a really magnificent classical dancer.

leave behind them, their tradition; it is a *corps de ballet* and the principals, the record they leave, their tradition; it is a repertoire, scores, designs. The Diaghileff Ballet could certainly have survived, if it had possessed roots; it had left Russia too far behind it for the amusing and unstable studio gossip of Paris. Diaghileff had the wit to guide his company through the dangers of dilettantism. His potential followers and lieutenants could not see through the shams that surrounded them. The Diaghileff public largely killed his ballet.

It is here that I come to this question of National Ballet,[1] a phrase I have used hitherto with no attempt at explanation and that must be defined before I can begin an analysis of the Wells company as it stands today. The future of the Wells as a creative force depends on its true understanding, especially when companies and dancers who are new and whose décors and costumes are less war-weary come to beguile us, and those who can only applaud a foreign label sigh with delight and say, as they surely will, 'After all these long years the ballet is with us once again.'

Again, let me add that I shall be the first to welcome them, their absence has left a void; only I shall say, 'The *Russian* Ballet is with us once again.'

[1] Let me make it quite clear that I have no wish to rename the Sadlers Wells Ballet. My use of the words National Ballet is to explain its functions and its future, its position in our national artistic life.

CHAPTER IV

NATIONAL BALLET

I. WHAT IS A NATIONAL BALLET?

WHAT is a national ballet and what are its functions? At first the answer seems too obvious for discussion, yet, at lectures I have given, it has aroused more heated questioning than any other topic.

The essential requisites of a national ballet are a fixed domicile, a school attached to the theatre and that the majority of the dancers and staff belong to the country of domicile.

The outstanding example is the 'Imperial-State' Ballet of Russia, which has survived every régime and has kept the art alive for the entire world. Diaghileff started his activities as its travelling branch. The ballet in Copenhagen is another fine example. The Paris Opéra was the original national ballet, but for many years it has not fulfilled one of the essential attributes of a national ballet, that of playing a real part in the artistic life of the nation. It has not stood for French art since the great days of the Romantic movement, and the engagement of an immature foreign choreographer, Lifar, as *maître de ballet* marked its lowest ebb.

The American Ballet, which started with a flourish of trumpets and a wealthy backer, might have found success had it gone about things the hard way with a young American choreographer at its head. In charge of the brilliant Balanchine, it became an expression of his very positive personality and so belied its name. Its American dancers were remarkable. No other nation has finer physical material nor a greater number of races and national themes upon which to draw. Faulty planning has delayed the structure as well as a snobbery about accepting the domestic product that is even worse than ours.

There must obviously be a guiding spirit in the national ballet; but continuity must be assured, and in a private enterprise this is only possible when a board of trustees can take the place of the state. But neither board nor state must interfere with artistic policy. In France it was otherwise; and 'protection' alone decided the casting of roles.

A national ballet must have in its permanent repertoire those 'museum' pieces that are the classical foundations of the art.

II. THE NATIONAL THEME IN BALLET

These points are all straightforward; the debatable question is how far should a national ballet exploit national themes. Is it necessary for it to adhere to a 'Buy British' policy? The very question seems to me an absurdity. Even were such a thing creatively possible, the public would not long stand for an un-varied diet of balletic roast beef and Yorkshire pudding. There can be no ruling on such a point. Creation must be spontaneous and the very fact of environment will of necessity create a number of 'national' ballets.

The Polish Ballet, formed just before the war, attempted an all-Polish programme—music, décor, theme, choreography—and the result was indescribably dull. The truly 'Russian' ballets produced by the early Diaghileff were *The Polovtsian Dances from Prince Igor*, *The Firebird*, *Petrouchka*, *Le Coq d'Or*, but his successes in-cluded *Les Sylphides*, *Le Spectre de la Rose*, *Carnaval*. Massine pro-duced only three 'Russian' ballets: *The Midnight Sun* and *Contes Russes*, both early works, and *Le Pas d'Acier*, which was Russia at second hand. His greatest success was *Le Tricorne*, the result of Spanish environment. Nijinska had one, *Les Noces* (she had but recently left Russia), and Balanchine none at all. Fokine, whose link with Russia was the closest, produced the most 'national' ballets. Yet even in the case of Diaghileff, who had worked on a definite artistic policy, these ballets were not deliberately planned as being national and the result of his travels can be seen in all his programmes. The admirable Philadelphia Ballet[1] produced two truly 'American' works, *Terminal* and *Barn Dance*, each more suc-cessful than the very deliberate attempts by the Russians to please and amuse England with *The Triumph of Neptune* and America with *Union Pacific*. The truly 'English' ballets in the Sadlers Wells repertoire are *Job*, *The Rake's Progress*, *The Prospect Before Us*, *Comus*, *Hamlet*, and in its mood and genre *Façade*.

The national theme should not be the aim of a national ballet; it will arise naturally and spontaneously out of it. And all the works produced by the company will bear traces more or less evident of

[1] London Hippodrome, June 1937.

their nationality, which is a point to be discussed later. For that very reason I have put the nationalities between inverted commas.

III. SADLERS WELLS AS THE NATIONAL BALLET

How far does Sadlers Wells fulfil the requisites of a national ballet?

It has a permanent home,[1] a school attached, an assured continuity, an all-British personnel, and it certainly has a definite place in British artistic life. It is also a museum for the great classical works.

The greatest problem is that of the school. It has already produced its own fine dancers and as a dancing academy has amply proved itself. But a national ballet requires more than a dancing school. The dancer may shine on the stage before the age of sixteen—Baronova, Toumanova and recently a dancer of altogether extraordinary ease and brilliance, Beryl Grey—but it is a sad thought if the dancer's general education is to cease before that age.

IV. PROBLEM OF THE IMMATURE DANCER

This is indeed the age of the immature dancer. The sixteen-year-old delights us every season with some brilliantly executed and seemingly well-interpreted role. We sense an important discovery and then a couple of seasons later are bitterly disappointed. The dancer has developed tiresome mannerisms; her smile is more like a grin, she is over-aware of her audience, her technique is still brilliant but a trifle forced. That is the history of over a dozen dancers of all nationalities. The reason is only too obvious. At sixteen she is not consciously interpreting the roles at all, though we credit her with interpretation. She takes pleasure in her dancing and she communicates that pleasure to us. She is not really aware of the difficulties. She is guided purely by instinct. Then she grows a little and begins to reason. She realises that there is such a thing as interpretation and sets out to interpret for all she is worth. She

---

[1] Remember that this is but one essential. A site in South Kensington does not create a national theatre even when backed by an influential committee. Lilian Baylis founded a truly national theatre and the fact should have been recognised before other plans were made.

realises that she is doing something difficult and begins to dread those notorious thirty-two *fouettés*. The audience has been flattering and has told her that she is now a serious rival to such-and-such a ballerina. She sets out to please the audience, fails, and both she and the audience wonder why. The instinct of a child who enjoys her dancing gives far finer results than the faulty reasoning of a semi-educated woman. That, to put it bluntly, is the only reason. No, not quite the only reason, for there is a physical as well as a psychological reason and the two are very closely related. The physical deterioration of the immature dancer is very noticeable, the result of strain and a faulty knowledge of hygiene. A school matron and a physician who understood the dancer's life would save many a promising dancer. The Russian dancer of the grand period, started on the right lines, did not deteriorate in physique or suffer from foot ailments. Kschesinska could dance and teach the whole day long at over sixty, and she was no exception. In the case of the travelling Russians it was a genuine case of over-work, which with us does not ordinarily arise. But the strain that could be corrected by sound education is very noticeable. Our national ballet, to succeed in the way that the Russian ballet has succeeded, must aim at establishing a boarding or even a day school in which a sound general education, one that stresses music and literature, will run parallel with the dancing. Only in this way shall we ever turn out dancers who are the peers of the Maryinsky ballerinas. Should this be impracticable, it should prove possible for the Wells to send its teachers to certain schools in the vicinity of London where their pupils might be sent.

Apart from a general education, the ballet school must pay attention to the drama. We hear a great deal about the value of movement in the actor's education. *The dancer is as much concerned with Stanislavsky as Cecchetti. The ballet is only interesting as a branch of the theatre, only the complete theatrical personality is interesting as a dancer.* It was so in the great days of ballet, it must be so today and in the future. Sadlers Wells has the one great chance of bringing that about, because it fits in with the English temperament, as all who have applauded *The Rake's Progress* will readily see.

These are schemes for post-war planning, but meanwhile it is a fact that several promising recruits are lost to ballet because their parents very rightly do not wish them to give up all education in their early teens.

V. NATIONAL CHARACTERISTICS IN DANCING

We now come to the question, Is there an English style of dancing? There is a clearly and easily distinguished Italian, French and Russian style of dancing. The first two are artistically obsolete and it is their blend, the Russian style, that survives today. The Russian Academy was founded in the middle of the eighteenth century, in the reign of the Empress Anne. The Russian style was born in the beginning of the twentieth century with that wonderful galaxy of ballerinas, Kschesinska, Trefilova, Preobrajenska, and later Pavlova and Karsavina. It will be seen that a national style is not developed under several generations. Also it took the combination of the teaching of the Italian Cecchetti and the Dane Johannsen, an exponent of the French method. The majority of our teachers are the direct pupils of Cecchetti (Italo-Russian) or of various Russian teachers. National physique, temperament and environment will undoubtedly develop an English school in time, but at present our one mature creation, Margot Fonteyn, is a pure exponent of the Russian style.

There are certain well-defined tendencies in the English dancer; in the classics a high aptitude for technique but a certain lack of stage-craft and interpretative ability. That is bound up with the problem of the immature dancer. The immature Russian dancer gets away with it through stage-craft, which is another term for legitimate bluff. In ballets such as *Carnaval* or *Les Sylphides*, the English girl either funks the delicate acting required or wallows in pertness and saccharin. It is in the acting of a positive dramatic role that the English dancer excels. It would be difficult to imagine a finer example of true mime than that of any cast in *The Rake's Progress*. Whether the dancers know their Hogarth or not, they certainly produce the illusion of a true familiarity with the period. This may be due to a certain national diffidence, the ability to perform well behind a mask.

These are of course generalisations and the English dancer has been the victim of many false generalisations by people—always the English themselves—who misuse such words as temperament, personality and glamour. Temperament, as I understand it in a theatrical sense, means the ability to suggest that the dancer is performing spontaneously and for pleasure and not running through a set piece. It does *not* mean the making of a great deal of noise and the pulling of grimaces as in certain pseudo-Spanish dances. Experience shows that as soon as the English girl finds her way in a company, she has as much temperament as the foreigner and often it is far more subtle in quality. A word to those who can see good only in the foreign dancer; temperament does not mean a continual series of quarrels with the management and the other dancers. That in any language is just bad manners.

Personality? First, to clear away a common misunderstanding. It does not mean the attracting of attention through something that is not in the book of words. To me in dancing it means the co-ordination of an intelligent mind and a responsive body. It may be a rare quality, it is not the monopoly of the foreigner. Massine has it, Helpmann has it, Baronova has it, Fonteyn has it, so have a few girls or boys in the *corps de ballet* of every company.

Glamour I refuse to discuss, it is altogether too abstract and meaningless, like fighting the wind. It damned the Russians in the name of the Italians and it has damned the English in the name of the Russians. Call Smith Popova and shout *brava!* In fifty years' time call Popova Smith and shout *brava!* again. So much for glamour.

In ballet it is not good form to use the word 'sex appeal', yet exist it does, and the very idea has so shocked the 'modern' as opposed to the ballet dancer that she has gone out of her way to wallow in ugliness of costume and make-up. Such an extreme consciousness of sex in ballet has never spread to the two ballet countries Russia and England. Their similarity of taste suggests possibilities of many interesting visits. I was able to enjoy a long conversation with a Soviet official whom I had met for the first time at a crowded party—both of us balancing tea-cups—on the subject of *The Swan Lake*.

VI. NATIONAL CHARACTERISTICS IN CHOREOGRAPHY

After these generalisations about English dancing, a few words on the choreography as apart from the ballet set on a national theme. Is there as yet an English style of choreography? Once again we must go to Russian ballet for examples. To the connoisseur, *Les Sylphides* is as Russian as *Petrouchka*; it contains the very essence of the Russian school of dancing. It is the artistic child of those first Russian ballets that were the result of the collaboration of

Petipa and Tchaikovsky. When some years ago I visited the Scala, Milan, I was amazed at the classical ballets I saw; it was a technique so very different, yet so slick and competent that I felt I was watching something totally unfamiliar. The choreography was nothing but an exploitation of that *staccato*, graceless acrobatic technique, and the dancers' legs would have supported a concert grand.

Choreography and dancing are closely related for the obvious reason that the choreographer can only use and exploit the material available, though a choreographer of strong personality can exert a powerful influence on dancing technique. Fokine is a striking example. The old-fashioned dancer could never have danced let alone interpreted *Le Spectre de la Rose* or the prelude in *Les Sylphides*, which is the very touchstone of romantic as opposed to classical dancing. It is in this prelude that the artist can be judged and not in the more spectacular *Blue Bird*, because in *Les Sylphides* the music dictates not merely the rhythm of the dance but the entire mood. As we have not yet had time to develop a 'school' of dancing, we have yet to develop a style of choreography. We have shown certain tendencies that I will discuss later in an analysis of our three choreographers. Let us remember that though we are writing of something that is in the direct line of a very great tradition, something that is destined to be an evolution and not a revolution, we are today at the very beginning of that evolution and cannot afford to be dogmatic about its direction. The time for a history of British ballet will not come for at least another fifty years; one can only write certain notes for the future historian.

CHAPTER V

THE AUDIENCE

APPRECIATION AND CRITICISM

I HAVE at various stages in this study used the words *entertainment* and *art*; I have also written a great deal about the audience. It might be useful to study certain types in that audience and to see what it is they expect in return for their modest fee.

There are the 'casuals' who want to see a show and who drift by accident[1] to the ballet, either with open minds or with hazy memories of Genée and Pavlova. I have recently made a nuisance of myself by questioning many such people. Their replies are interesting and deserve respect.

In general it is the *ballet blanc* that they like. It completely fulfils what they expect of ballet, an easy relationship between music and dancing, graceful movement and enough pointwork to satisfy a natural craving for a technical display. They are aware of the dancing, the choreography means nothing to them; in some cases they imagine it to be a kind of improvisation. The most inexperienced theatregoer is conscious of the author's role, largely ignores the producer's and is mainly concerned with the actor's. The tyro-balletgoer concentrates his attention entirely on the dancer.

If he has enjoyed himself—he may of course have been bored— then his pleasure is extreme. Ballet is the last stronghold of theatrical illusion and for two hours he has escaped from reality. He knows and feels nothing of the sweat and hard work required and has no doubts as to the perfect interpretation of the work. On many occasions in the past I have heard a little gasp, 'Pavlova! how wonderful!' when some definitely second-rate dancer came onto the stage and, until the real Pavlova appeared and revealed herself to the most obtuse, the spectator was completely happy. Only Pavlova had made him into a critic.

Alas, after the beginner has been a few times, he begins to distinguish between performers and to pick up a smattering of

[1] Not so easy when House Full is the rule.

technical jargon. The first illusion is gone for ever, to be succeeded by the thrill of growing knowledge. He then knows that he prefers A to X; she is more graceful, prettier, has a stronger technique; this last, which may or may not be true, gives him enormous pleasure. 'Technique' is a password, it makes him into a *balletomane*.

He next follows his few chosen personalities through the various ballets in the repertoire, which he judges solely by the opportunities it gives them. Hence that phrase, 'there is no dancing in this ballet', which might be translated 'I have not had an opportunity of watching A undisturbed by other movement'.

When he has reached the stage of talking about an *entrechat* or a *fouetté* his education is complete, and he then allows himself the liberty of calling his favourites by their Christian names. 'Bobby' was wonderful tonight; Tamara's *fouettés* are better than Irina's; and so on *ad nauseam*.

What the few enthusiasts of this type really see in ballet that induces them to come night after night is a matter for the psychologist and need not concern us here.

For what does the true connoisseur look? That is a question worth attempting to answer. It can give us a standard by which the current repertoire may be judged and I suggest that it should be studied in the light of what follows; only then can this satisfactory report of the National Ballet be truly appreciated. His quest is for completeness. Ballet is a composite art, and it is only when its component parts are in harmony that the result is completely satisfying.

There is a series of questions that he asks himself. What has the choreographer set out to do? Was it worth doing? Has he succeeded? The answers may be more or less complicated. The simplicity of the first rather depends on the producer. It is, however, a very common error to criticise the choreographer because he has not attempted something entirely different, something that the critic wished him to do. The answer to the second is more a matter of opinion; the third involves further questions. Was his aim consistently followed through? Was the relationship between music, décor, dancing and drama a true one? And finally, the most personal question of all, Was my interest maintained throughout?

Let us examine a very familiar work in this manner; *Les Sylphides*, which is so well known that we have ceased to think about it at all.

The choreographer's aim was to create a romantic atmosphere through the interpretation of certain music of Chopin. It was worth doing for a number of obvious reasons and for the historical reason that it had never been done before. Fokine took the essence of romantic ballet and dispensed with the tedious and unconvincing claptrap of romanticism. He has succeeded because the technique used is so simple that no problems of execution divert the attention from the atmosphere which is maintained throughout, because there is no conventional *corps de ballet* but a group of dancers all of whom interpret the music. The relationship between music, movement, atmosphere and décor, the one by Benois used originally by Fokine and now adopted by the Wells, is a true one, each expressing something parallel in emotion. Personally my interest has always been maintained throughout, and that is the case with 99·9 per cent of any audience.

That and nothing more technical or that requires the use of jargon is the basis of all criticism and appreciation. It may be necessary to see a work several times with different artists and under different conditions for such a test to be applied fairly. My main point is that only after the ballet has been considered as a whole does the connoisseur turn his attention to the dancing. Having decided what was the choreographer's aim, he asks himself if the dancers have made it apparent and done it justice. If the choreographer's aim was to show off a series of *fouettés*, a poor aim, then he may discuss those *fouettés* to his heart's content. But let there be no mistake, in the ballroom act of *Swan Lake* there is more to the ballerina role than a series of 32 *fouettés*.[1] Petipa wishes to contrast Odette and Odile, the one a princess under a spell, the other a hard and brilliant sorceress. Those *fouettés* are merely a device to show how dazzling the sorceress can be, adopted by Petipa because they were difficult and consequently fashionable at the time. However perfect, they cannot make the role. That is merely one example in the criticism of dancing which is not as simple as it seems nor yet as complicated a mystery as the 'high-priest fan' tries to make out.

The connoisseur is a constant visitor because of that quest for completeness and perfection. He realises that no two performances are ever the same, that the variation is very great indeed.

[1] In St. Petersburg they were the *clou* of the act, today because of the advance in technique they pass largely unnoticed.

Mr Agate, who admits that he dislikes ballet, will watch trotting horses for hours in search of perfection of movement; he is a connoisseur of horses. It is strange that such a man with his rare understanding of acting and theatrical tradition and his love of music should be blind to ballet. I suspect that he has been listening to a section of the public I have described instead of watching the stage, or that he has chosen his programmes badly. I admit that his prejudice rattles me, for whether he writes of Bernhardt or golf he has long been a favourite bedside author—his *Ego* would be a great stand-by on a desert island— and his unprejudiced remarks could have been of immense benefit to ballet. His standards of fine acting, his refusal to follow the Bergner hysteria, are a convincing proof of that. If he is wilfully ignorant of ballet, the average ballet-lover knows disgracefully little about the stage in general. I am never tired of repeating that ballet is a branch of the theatre —music critics kindly note—and that to confine one's interest to the dance alone is to lose sight of it altogether.

CHAPTER VI

THREE CHOREOGRAPHERS

I. DIFFICULTIES OF CHOREOGRAPHY

THE choreographer has always been a rarity in ballet. In the rich annals of the Imperial Russian Ballet one man, Marius Petipa, dominated a half-century and with all his resources Diaghileff was only able to use Fokine and to 'discover' Nijinsky, Massine, Nijinska and Balanchine. De Basil developed Lichine, who truly had the gift but who required the most careful handling in order to develop it to the full.

When one considers the nature of choreography that is not astonishing. There can be no school apart from experience. Choreography is in part the dancer's reaction against the set exercises of the classroom, but in order to make such a reaction effective the choreographer requires a thorough knowledge of the mechanics of dancing, a conductor's knowledge of the score, a producer's knowledge of the theatre and must also have something of the make-up of a painter-sculptor. Since he is working in a living medium he must be at any rate an instinctive psychologist. Noverre recognised and outlined these many essential attributes, and even added a knowledge of geometry.

It is amazing that in this short time we in England have developed a number of choreographers, two of whom are major figures, and a third who must be taken very seriously indeed, though there has been a tendency to dignify every dancer who arranges a few dances by the appellation 'choreographer'. Our major figures are Frederick Ashton, Ninette de Valois and through one work, *Hamlet*, Robert Helpmann, while Andrée Howard, examples of whose work I would like to see at the Wells, and Anthony Tudor[1] have done some inconsistent but really interesting work, and Wendy Toye has shown true musical taste and an

---

[1] Anthony Tudor has recently had his greatest success in America and we have not seen his latest and most ambitious work. His *Jardin aux Lilas* showed tremendous promise.

original outlook. Keith Lester has produced many works for various companies, the most ambitious being *David* for Markova-Dolin. This is an imposing list.

II. FREDERICK ASHTON

Although still in his prime, Ashton can be considered the father of English choreography; that statement shows the extreme youth of our ballet.

I have already outlined his background. The prentice choreographer is greatly influenced by the dancers at his disposal and Ashton was fortunate in having available Marie Rambert's brilliant and eager little group. *Capriol Suite, Mars and Venus, Leda, The Lady of Shalott, Florentine Picture* were the first results. These ballets revealed an extraordinary fluency, true elegance and real wit. Their very finish precluded any great inventiveness in steps and the small group he was working with made him excel in the *pas de deux* and *pas seul* rather than in massed movement. Then came the Camargo Society and the opportunity to work with the accomplished classical ballerina Markova, both there and at the Ballet Club. The results were *Pomona, Façade, La Péri, Les Masques, Le Foyer de la Danse* and *Mephisto Waltz*.

Pomona gave him for the first time the opportunity of using a *corps de ballet, La Péri* of showing off a virtuoso. The Ashton of that period was in danger of stagnating through the very ease with which he created. He was scarcely ever 'promising', he seemed to have arrived from the very first. *Les Masques*, brilliantly decorated by Fedorovitch, was a case in point, witty, polished but somehow dated from the very beginning, and impersonal. It was a neo-Diaghileff ballet. This easy success failed to satisfy Ashton or those who had followed his rapid development, though when he joined the young Wells Ballet many thought he was making a serious mistake, through identifying himself with anything so far removed from the West End. The use of a stable company, another argument in favour of national ballet, gave him his chance, which he used to create *Les Rendezvous, Les Patineurs, Apparitions, Le Baiser de la Fée, Nocturne, Harlequin in the Street, Wedding Bouquet* and *Horoscope*.

Les Rendezvous had all his accustomed wit and elegance with something added. To start with it was dancer-proof; change the cast a dozen times and it remains first class. The fact that it has not dated is obvious. It has become a permanent acquisition; the perfect curtain-raiser.

Ashton had already shown his ability as a true romantic, on a small scale, in *The Lady of Shalott* and *The Mephisto Valse*, while in *Apparitions* he inaugurated a phase of romantic choreography, meeting the competition of Fokine's *Don Juan* and later *Paganini*, Nijinska's *La Bien Aimée* and *Legend of Cracow*, and Massine's *Symphonie Fantastique*. And his work stood the comparison, his simple ballroom scene, the most complete and perfect example of the new romanticism, showing a remarkable feeling for its very essence as apart from its more conventional props. Lambert's selection from Liszt, brilliantly orchestrated by Gordon Jacob, was in itself an outstanding achievement. In *Le Baiser de la Fée* Ashton in his movements echoed the relationship between Stravinsky and Tchaikovsky, between Petipa and the new choreography, a parallelism with the score that was particularly happy. I remember a very beautiful adagio and variation that bore the unmistakable signature of Ashton. He had shaken off the many natural influences of the early days. *Nocturne* is another outstanding work, a deeply moving choreographic poem and a sensitive translation of a very elusive composer, Delius. Ashton produces with such apparent ease and immediate effectiveness that one is apt to overlook his subtlety and it is only when his work is really well known that it appears; the Polka in *Façade*, for instance, with its laugh at the dignity of the classical dancer; for that reason I resent the immediate laugh raised by the totally unnecessary corsets. The subtlety of *Façade* is revealed by the fact that it is not as immediately popular as one would think in camps where the majority of the audience is seeing ballet for the first time. *Les Rendezvous* is subtle, particularly in the way in which the separate dancers in the suite are joined together, and the dancers are characterised with all the speed and economy of a lightning sketch. The curtain in *Nocturne* is a subtle summary of the whole ballet. Even *Les Patineurs*, seemingly obvious at first sight, has innumerable touches that reveal the most careful observation and a construction that is in fact very far from obvious. Just because Ashton's subtlety is purely plastic and never literary, it is impossible for the critic to write about it at length without making a fool of himself, through discovering a thousand and one things never intended by the creator. I have committed a number of critical sins while learning ballet, but never that particular one.

Ashton has the most plastic sense of all our choreographers. *Wedding Bouquet*, essentially a literary jest, is no exception; Ashton has translated it into movement. This work may displease many, but it is worthy to go into the Diaghileff repertoire that produced *Les Biches* and would completely show up such shallow and ephemeral works as the once popular *Le Train Bleu* and *Ode*. Massine alone can exploit such an infinite variety of moods, Balanchine alone has such a light touch. I am making no direct comparisons, they would lead us nowhere.

In his war–time productions Ashton has found a new depth of emotion, proving those who saw him as brilliant but superficial to be wrong, as a study of *Nocturne* and passages in *Le Baiser de la Fée* and *Apparitions* should have done.

The Wise and Foolish Virgins might seem at first a fine school piece. It is far more than that, it is one of Ashton's major works, one of those rare pieces of choreography so perfectly musical, so delicately balanced that one could not imagine a movement or a gesture altered. It is difficult with such a work, which is fine ballet as well as fine choreography, to separate music, movement and decoration; they form a perfect whole. Its grouping, which is particularly beautiful, is never underlined at the expense of the whole, it occurs perfectly naturally out of the music. The more one sees this particular work the more exquisite detail is revealed. Ashton here carries forward the work begun in *The Florentine Picture* and shows that he has assimilated a knowledge of Italian painting until he can use it with perfect freedom. This ballet is moving through its simple beauty.

In *Dante Sonata* he is powerfully moving, even harrowing. He uses what has become known as the symphonic technique to startling effect; that same technique that had become as worn as the conventional miming of the classics. Even the theme, the combat between good and evil, seemed threadbare. Yet this whole work has a pitch of intensity, foreshadowed by that other major work *Horoscope*, that it would seem impossible to maintain. He not only maintains it, but works up to a powerful climax. And here one must mention the remarkable instrument that the Wells company has become, unique in modern ballet as a *team* of dancers. In *The Green Table* Jooss, one of the most interesting figures in the contemporary dance, shows the impact of war through a semi-realistic approach; his triumph is in the more passive scenes around the green table itself. Ashton shows the suffering of the spirit, the martyrdom of humanity, giving the spectator a genuine experience, a rarity in the modern theatre. It was directly inspired by the sufferings of Poland.

The Wanderer has been hailed as his masterpiece, a view I do not share, though it contains passages of striking beauty, and as a musical interpretation is always more interesting than Balanchine's treatment in *Errantes*, though (this is a personal view) it does not coincide with my feeling of the music. Much as I admire Graham Sutherland as an artist, I do not find that the costumes express the mood of the music or the movement, and they are distracting enough to interfere with the effect. Ashton is undoubtedly the choreographer for the semi-abstract ballet; but such work requires the closest collaboration with the decorative artist. I would like to see this work re-dressed—by Sutherland himself but in closer collaboration with Ashton. In the *Dante Sonata* Sophie Fedorovitch, taking her inspiration from Flaxman, has given such collaboration, also in *Nocturne*, her greatest work. Where movement is complex, costume and décor must be simple, if the pattern is to remain clear.

The study of Ashton cannot in any sense be considered final, even up to the present period, and it is for the many who have followed his work to amplify these notes from their own experience. As I have already suggested, he is an intricate artist to write of because of the very direction his gifts have taken. He has travelled the most difficult path of all, from successful elegance and slickness to depth and subtlety, from glitter and prettiness to brilliance and beauty. He has had every opportunity to be spoilt but he has gone about things the hard way, developing from ballet to ballet. He has enhanced the national ballet, but it alone has made the fruition of his talent possible. Working with a large international company, he could not have failed to have gained success, but at the expense of permanency, and much of his work is permanent repertoire material; an addition to the museum that national ballet becomes.

In his latest work, *The Quest*, an exceptionally distinguished collaboration with William Walton and John Piper, he invokes a national theme from Edmund Spenser.

The Quest is undoubtedly the work of a master who can make a rich and varied use of the classical idiom, and though the work belongs to the 'made' rather than to the inspired group the perfect collaboration shown makes it worthy of Diaghileff in his great days.

Of our three major choreographers he is the least specifically English and most in the direct Russo-international tradition. He develops his characterisation through 'aria' rather than 'recitative' dancing, taking his place alongside the successors to the great Fokine.

III. NINETTE DE VALOIS

This Admirable Crichton of the ballet world has been dancer, pedagogue, manager and choreographer and at times lecturer and author. Her book *Invitation to the Dance*, aggressive and involved as it is in places, is the one book necessary for the serious student among the hundred or so produced. No one interested in ballet as an art can afford to miss the writings of someone who has studied every branch. It is with her choreography that we are here concerned, though we cannot forget those other functions in the background which must have limited her choreographic output considerably. All our three choreographers, so different in outlook and method, have this in common, a wide general education before they started choreography. Ashton came to ballet late, de Valois danced for many years, Helpmann acted, danced and travelled. I have no faith in the pupil-choreographer or in his ability to tell the public anything new. Choreography is essentially an art for the mature.

Apart from her successful experience as a dancer and her mechanical knowledge as a teacher, de Valois' grounding was as a theatrical producer, where she had to produce effective choral grouping with non-dancers. She started out as a rebel against both classicism and its ultra-modern application. The first result that I saw was *Rout*, which can be best described as what every rebel at that period was doing, 'much sound and fury, signifying nothing'. Her slighter efforts were very slight indeed. As a teacher in those days she seemed to me to drill all the individuality out of her pupils. The pre-Camargo de Valois was interesting only as a dancer who seemed to have thrown away a career. That was, of course, only on the surface, so that the immediate success of *Job* came as a total surprise. In it she showed a fine knowledge of music and all that she had learnt through her connection with the Abbey and the Festival Theatres. She also pointed a totally new choreographic direction, one that was the exact opposite to that of Ashton. In terms of painting she was becoming a master of the *Conversation Piece*. Her point of departure was the most risky of all, literature, literature inspired by painting at that. I have already outlined those difficulties, insuperable unless one has a strong musical knowledge and understands and feels the mechanics of dancing.

De Valois' work can be divided into two groups, the first suggested by painting or by a literary conception—*Job*, *The Rake's Progress*, *The Prospect Before Us*, *Checkmate*, *The Gods Go A-Begging* (Watteau); the second by the music or by a more conventional 'ballet story', *Prometheus*, *The Haunted Ballroom*, *Les Douanes*, *Barabau*.

The test of the first group is, Is the style consistent? Is the dancing interesting in itself, and does it develop character? Does the ballet illustrate episodes in the story or really tell it without the need of continual reference to the programme? (Some people will always bury their heads in the programme in a plucky effort to discover to which of the girls the young man in *Les Sylphides*[1] is engaged. We will ignore them.)

They are magnificently consistent in style and fulfil Fokine's definition of balletic naturalism. One has only to call to mind in *The Rake's Progress* the entrance of the young girl which establishes her character, her needlework dance which develops it, the dancing-master's dance, the gambler's and the rope dance, all taken at random, to see how she builds up character and maintains interest in the dances themselves. In *Checkmate* I have only to mention the Black and Red Queens or the Knights to answer both questions again. The stories are magnificently clear visually, even the involved *Prospect Before Us* is possible without the volume in the programme, though it is the least easy. In *Checkmate* the narrative is told with a suspense worthy of *The Arabian Nights*. Given a positive and powerful subject that can be told in direct narrative, de Valois has no equal. With the exception of *The Gods Go A-Begging*, she is less happy with trivialities; she has little ballet small-talk.

[1] This happens to be true, as is also an ingenious version of *Le Spectre de la Rose*: 'She dances with the gardener; he hears her father coming and jumps out of the window'. I am indebted to my friend Wesley Hooper for this gem.

This *Gods Go A-Begging* is especially interesting. There have been three versions by Balanchine, de Valois and Lichine, each one equally charming, though the Balanchine *pas de deux* is outstanding. Each one bears a strong resemblance to the others, though no three personalities could differ more strongly and there is no suggestion of plagiarism. Some music imposes its treatment, and in this case all three works are as good as the essentially logical score. The *Haunted Ballroom* was a first-class production; its choreography is no better than the music. *Les Douanes* was funny and when she herself danced in it had a certain elegance and wit, but without her it was 'oh-la-la-humour' at its weakest and a worthy curtain-raiser to that very successful comedy, *French Without Tears*. *Prometheus* I admired, particularly the children's *rondo*, but its costumes were a handicap and, should anyone tell me it dragged in parts, I would be inclined to agree. *Barabau* with its clever score, costumes and scenery, trivial though it was, succeeded in being a genuine *ballet bouffe* after a comparative failure by Balanchine with similar material.

When de Valois chooses the right material, Cruikshank and Callot, Goya and Greenaway await her, she produces something that will live. Quite apart from her work as its creator, guide and inspirer, her ballets have justified the name National Ballet and will become its most valuable exports.

IV. ROBERT HELPMANN

After gaining fame as an actor-dancer, Helpmann has turned choreographer and has produced three very individual works. It would ordinarily be too soon to discuss him as a choreographer had not one of those works, *Hamlet*, shown an entirely new tendency, something that separates him from any other worker in the medium and forms a strong contrast to those opposites Ashton and de Valois. Unlike Ashton, his work reveals a national tendency; unlike de Valois, he arrives at it from a totally different angle. The three working together give to the Wells *a variety of outlook that no company has ever possessed*. Had any but an English company been in the hands of three choreographers, the result would have been another 'Bullet in the Ballet'. One at a time has always been the rule.

His first ballet, *Comus*, like most first ballets, was in a sense a reflection of his own capabilities and I cannot well see it revived without him. He has adapted the old English art form of the masque, using speech as a part of the action yet never holding up the action for the sake of speech. That is especially noteworthy. The speech is an innovation in contemporary ballet, it comes as a surprise, but it is a legitimate device and never in any sense a stunt. Its use has attracted undue attention. He tells his narrative in a straightforward manner and develops his characters remarkably well. The dancing is simple and he has not attempted, beginner-like, to show everything he knows. The grouping is superb and occurs entirely naturally. These are important but mainly negative qualities. The positive qualities are the suggestion of an unreal world, the dancing of Sabrina and the blend of speech with movement. Its one flaw consists in a too limited repertoire of movement. When he suggests the 'light fantastic round', the ensuing dance has little fantasy to match the poetry.

As a ballet this would merit a permanent place in the repertoire, that is if any other dancer but Helpmann could speak on the stage. I have once heard the attempted acting of a prominent male dancer and the result leads me to wish never to hear anything of the kind again.

The next ballet, *Hamlet*, accomplished something entirely new, nothing less than a commentary on Shakespeare, a commentary that could not have been made in any other medium. To tell a Shakespearian story, as has been done with *Hamlet* before and recently in *Twelfth Night*, is out of place in ballet. Shakespeare's stories are nothing paraphrased and far too involved to be suitable as ballets. To use them is purely to profit by the name, a short-sighted policy at that, for it damns the producer in any intelligent critic's eyes.

Both Helpmann and de Valois have sought literary inspiration, but they have never been swamped by literature, they have *translated* their stories into the dance medium and produced something that is parallel to the literature and the music. With great skill Helpmann fixed on the lines

> For in that sleep of death what dreams may come
> When we have shuffled off this mortal coil,
> May give us pause.

The ballet begins with Hamlet's death, takes us through the frenzied delirium of his dying moments and closes with his death.

The most fervent Shakespearian could not quarrel with the method. In this delirium Helpmann suggests modern psychological explanations for Hamlet's actions—the identification of the Queen with Ophelia, jealousy of Laertes and Ophelia and the like. But, quite apart from this programme, the ballet itself is a magnificent theatrical spectacle. It is also the most vivid example of the really important role that décor can play in modern ballet; it embellishes classicism, but in the Fokine and post-Fokine ballet it has an active part. Here Leslie Hurry, a true discovery as a decorative artist, as his work on the new *Swan Lake* will show, has formed a link between Tchaikovsky's romanticism and Helpmann's essentially modern interpretation. From whatever angle we view it, this is a great and memorable ballet. It suggests a new range of choreography. Hitherto ballet has dealt with a narrative, *The Rake's Progress*; an atmosphere, *Les Sylphides*; a theme, *Les Biches*; or with the mechanics of movements beautiful in themselves, *The Sleeping Princess*. Here it has been made to provide a poetical commentary on a work of art in another medium. It is not necessary to add with what caution such an angle must be approached or to point its many pitfalls. It is either first class or a pathetic and pretentious failure. Helpmann, a potential stage Hamlet, obviously a student of the play, has made it into a success. Another word of warning: the critic of such works, and by that I mean the serious spectator, must not read into them more than they actually contain. It would be absurd to put the critical content above the spectacle or the atmosphere produced. The true nature of the ballet medium must be thoroughly understood, its power of suggestion, its weakness in any but the simplest of direct narratives. It would be absurd to talk of great Shakespearian criticism and to try and convey it into words. The beauty of the work is that its commentary is strictly in its own medium of movement.

An extraordinary fallacy has cropped up once again in connection with *Hamlet*. Its success is tremendous; the quality of Greek Tragedy that it possesses has been felt by those who knew nothing of *Hamlet*, but people have said with a certain disappointment that it contained little or no dancing. I cannot understand such an attitude over thirty years after Fokine defined the new ballet. *Hamlet* is obviously all dancing, it can be nothing else. It so happens that ballet like dancing has its *arias* and *recitatives*, and in *Hamlet* there are few *arias*, but it would be a sad thing if *arias* alone were recognised as music. The position is identical in ballet. English ballet apart from Ashton tends toward the *recitative*. The distinction between dancing and mime only existed in those classical ballets where long mimed scenes tried to cram the story in as a sort of afterthought between a virtuoso adagio and a virtuoso variation while the music went on in its own sweet way. There it was possible to talk of mimed scenes as opposed to dancing. *Fokine a changé tout cela*, today all mime is a part of the main structure, *i.e.* related to the musical rhythm and content. The mimed scene is only legitimate in the classical revival or in some pastiche.[1]

As if stung by this criticism, Helpmann's next work, *The Birds*, was mainly *aria*. It' has not the pretension to be anything more than a charming unsubstantial opening of a programme. It is good, very good even, though Ashton handles such froth with greater spontaneity. Helpmann has, perhaps by way of challenge, overcomplicated the steps, so that the effect depends on a perfect coordination of four dancers that cannot always be achieved. Yet *The Birds* has wit, characterisation and true style. Once again the decorative artist, Chiang Yee, has made the work a complete collaboration and his bird costumes show a freshness rare in this very hackneyed subject.

V. COLLABORATION OF MUSIC AND DÉCOR

These three ballets are a convincing proof of the need for careful planning, only possible when a company has a fixed domicile: Diaghileff (Monte Carlo), The Wells (London).

Lambert has assured the soundness of the musical planning in a programme that is unmatched. As a composer, a conductor, a critic and a musical director he has reconciled those often warring elements music and movement, doing violence to neither. I suggest

[1] Incidentally since writing this I was struck by the fact that the famous Act II of *Coppélia* contains the very minimum of dancing. This is, of course, a pre-Fokine ballet so that the statement is fully justified. It has two very short dances sandwiched in between a great deal of funny business. Some of the music is expressive of the pantomime, *e.g.* the pouring-out of the wine, but whole passages of real beauty, such as where Swanhilda is wheeled in, are completely wasted. This ballet shows better than anything the work accomplished by Fokine. He was responsible for a revival of it, and he quoted it to me as an example of a work in which it was justified because of its period to include mime that was distinct from dancing.

that the reader turn to the appendix on page 88 and study it carefully. That alone would give the Wells an international reputation.

In his three painters Oliver Messel, Leslie Hurry and Chiang Yee, Helpmann has been equally fortunate. It is often said by those who do not understand ballet in the Fokine sense of the word that the test of good choreography is its equal brilliance in practice costume. That is not at all the case. It may and it should have a meaning in practice costume, but in good modern ballet I cannot admit that the three elements can be separated.

There was a vivid example of that truth when *Les Présages* was given in practice costume against a cyclorama at Covent Garden as a result of protests against its décor and costumes. The experiment proved that the work lost considerably and that Masson's work, even if it lent itself to criticism, was playing its part in the general result. *Choreartium* was improved when given in practice dress, solely because the décor and costumes were sufficiently bad to hinder the work by getting between the choreographer and the audience. Imagine *Schéhérazade*, which forms a magnificent choreographic pattern, often unnoticed because of its drama, without the vital part played by Bakst. Imagine *Les Sylphides* in practice black! This austerity ballet notion, whether it seeks to dispense with décors or orchestra, is plain rubbish. *Ballet is not a synonym for dancing*.

Other examples of such close collaboration may be seen in *Dante Sonata* with Fedorovitch's designs, with McKnight Kauffer in *Checkmate* and with Rex Whistler in *The Wise Virgins*. Alter these and you destroy the work. In ballet the whole matters; let us once and for all forget dancing–choreography–music–décor and try and think of

Let us remember that concentration on dancing killed ballet for several generations, concentration on music and décor injured it so badly that the dancing of *The Sleeping Princess* (Alhambra, 1921)

was improperly appreciated, and a complete re-education of the public was necessary.

English painting has not yet had an opportunity of making use of the ballet medium, the fresco as Diaghileff once said, of the contemporary artist. I would like to see added to the list that contains Burra, Hurry, Piper, Sutherland, such names as Henry Moore, Frances Hodgkins, Ivon Hitchins, to name but three artists each of whom has something important to express through the medium of ballet. I have a long list of Australian artists who could gain an overdue reception to this country through the national ballet, and there are many interesting composers whose work deserves an international audience. There is no need to force a national theme, but there are themes in plenty.

It is in helping to bring about such artistic collaboration that the admirable C.E.M.A. has an important role to play. C.E.M.A., in fact, appears to be the perfect British compromise, a Ministry of Fine Arts without the politics or the red tape. So long as it assists, encourages, makes possible but does not manage theatrical enterprises it will be invaluable.

CHAPTER VII

THE CLASSICAL REPERTOIRE

I HAVE stressed the importance of the classics to the national ballet; without them there can be no complete dancer.

Sadlers Wells has rescued for Western Europe *Giselle*, *The Swan Lake, Casse-Noisette, The Sleeping Princess* and *Coppélia*, each in its original and unabbreviated form. We can now see how incomplete Odette is without Odilia and what has so often been regarded and misinterpreted as sister to *Les Sylphides* becomes a different work, diamond-hard and sparkling as well as romantic. It makes the use of 'Sylphides arms' impossible. It also brings back one of the most beautiful classical *pas de trois*[1] in the repertoire. Petipa in patchwork had become part of a school curriculum or an excuse for applauding a favourite dancer. We now see him as a complete artist and can understand more of the structure of ballet. We can even see the eternal *Sylphides*, often so admirably performed by the Wells, in a new light, not as a classic in the period sense of the word, but as a neo-romantic ballet. In a conversation with the author, Fokine was much amused at the description 'classic' applied to his *Les Sylphides*, since it was created as a romantic reaction away from classicism, just as *The Dying Swan* was a romantic reaction from such a composition as *Bluebird*, and the little drama *Le Spectre de la Rose* a manifesto of his neo-romanticism. He underlined the practical importance of keeping this clear. The danger, however, is not of Fokine being performed in the classical manner, but of the classics being performed in the Fokine manner. Most moderns have fallen into this trap with the exception of Markova, Gollner and recently Fonteyn.

Giselle, which I have discussed at length elsewhere, has formed Margot Fonteyn. It has played its part in making Helpmann into the complete actor. Its solitary survival from the Gautier period is interesting, since the music is definitely not the reason. It is the only ballet to survive on account of its story, or more accurately its theme, which sets the dancer the problem of interpreting the

---

[1] The stylish performance of this by a number of casts has shown more clearly than anything the scholastic success of the Wells.

body in Act I, the spirit in Act II. It is the 'type story' of the whole period but simplified and shorn of most of the trapdoor details that would cause laughter today. I strongly object to its being called the *Hamlet* of ballet. To do so shows no sense of proportion. It can only be so called in that it is the greatest dramatic test of the ballerina as *Hamlet* is of the tragedian. *Hamlet* impresses with adequate acting, anything but a great performance of *Giselle* is intolerable. It is that kind of work. To call it *La Dame au Camélias* of ballet would be more correct.

Coppélia has none of the grandeur of the other classics, but it is a wonderful vehicle for light comedy, and supported by Delibes' sparkling score it is well worthy of survival. Its disconnected and dramatically absurd third act is especially interesting to the student, revealing as it does all the ineptitudes of the banal and uninspired choreography that Fokine was to fight and destroy. In such small doses it has all the charm of Victorian bric-à-brac, while one dance in particular, *La Prière*, is a veritable Albert Memorial of choreography. A museum requires an example of such work.

In time these works, redecorated as in the case of *The Swan Lake*, by artists who can respect the tradition yet banish the effect of moth-balls, will be viewed with still greater pleasure and profit.

Leslie Hurry's designs for *The Swan Lake* constitute a work of major importance. It will be the first time that this great work has been seen here with décor as an equal partner, the first great restaging of a classic by our national ballet and the most ambitious classical revival since the Diaghileff-Bakst *Sleeping Princess*, 1921.

The success of Hurry's designs lies in the fact that he has brought an original mind to bear on an old work which he has obviously studied with care, and has at the same time paid scrupulous respect to tradition and to the type of movements the dancers have to perform. This setting will reveal a classic in a new light, allowing us to see to the full the amazing beauty of Petipa's choreography and forming a link with Tchaikovsky's score. *Hamlet* followed by *The Swan Lake* shows that the Wells (the discovery was Helpmann's) have not merely hit on a good décor, and many easel artists can produce something good, but on a real theatre artist, very rare since Diaghileff. Other classics await him.

The early Diaghileff dancers, Karsavina, Lopokova and Nijinsky, had all been trained in the classics; an abbreviated *Swan Lake* and an *Aurora's Wedding*, re-stated by the brilliant but very personal Nijinska, are insufficient training for either dancers or audience, and once again I must insist on the important role of the audience.

CHAPTER VIII

THE DANCERS

I. THE ARTIST-DANCER

I DO not intend to survey the company as a whole or to deal with every one of the many dancers of promise; to do so would date this book within a few months. I have already discussed the worrying problem of the immature dancer. It has struck me vividly on re-reading old press notices, and yet on the actual performances I was recording the truth. I should have qualified every remark by the word 'seemingly' or 'apparent'. In no other form of theatre does the problem exist in such an acute form.

The artist-dancer is in a very small minority, and although the profession as a whole appears to have a certain glamour, the average dancer reveals as little art and as much painstaking hard work as the average shop-girl or typist. We make a grave mistake, if we think otherwise. All we ask of her is to be attractive in appearance, reasonably musical and to keep her wits about her on the stage. She is an essential part of the whole; so is the filing clerk. The complete dancer requires other gifts which I have discussed on so many occasions. She needs a type of physique not often found in this country, it is far more common in America, and an altogether exceptional musical sense, something over and above the merely negative one of a good sense of rhythm. She has to be an accomplished actress. Lately I have learned to add something that I did not include previously; she needs a proper education, if she is to develop into a genuine artist. It is possible to be an artist-dancer without being a ballerina, but the misuse of that term has caused a great deal of harm. The title must be earned as any Russian knows. Call an unfledged dancer a *ballerina* and you cause her damage. The National Ballet has produced many fine dancers, one has only to think of June Brae and Pamela May; it has many promising dancers, among them the fluent Beryl Grey, the witty Dale, Moyra Fraser, Joan Sheldon and a number of others; it has produced but one *prima ballerina* who has been truly tested.

II. MARGOT FORTEYN

When Markova left the Wells the company remained without a ballerina. It is a mistake to imagine that a company cannot exist without a ballerina; that is, a well-planned company. It was not long, however, before a young dancer started to attract attention. She was perfect in build and appearance and she had an extraordinarily musical sensitivity. Her dancing was infinitely pleasing in *Les Sylphides* but lacked the necessary brilliance and authority in the classics that she had inherited from Markova.

The story of Margot Fonteyn has been one of consistent progress from season to season and with no relapse save for a forced smile during one particular season of strain. It was soon remedied by a dancer who listened to criticism rather than praise. Her first triumph was in Act I of *Giselle*, and she next added to it the second act, becoming one of those rare dancers who can reconcile the two. She danced Odette appealingly, then added to it Odile, proving that she could be hard and brilliant. After three seasons she danced Aurora as an experienced ballerina, yet could depict the pathos of the pricked finger, the first injury in a pampered life. She proceeded to classicism through romanticism, a point that I find important, since it has given her a range denied to so many great exponents of the classics.[1] There are many small details in her *Swan Lake* that give warm life to what might be a museum piece. I have seen it better danced in cases where those 32 *fouettés* formed the climax if not the *raison d'être* of the performance; I have never seen the role more fully explored as to character. Yet it is never fussy, there is no 'business', it all arises out of the music. With such a musical dancer *Les Sylphides* is the perfect ballet; one wishes that she might dance the prelude as well as the valse. Only in *Casse-Noisette* where the ballerina role is all fireworks and no character is she at her least successful. In *Casse-Noisette* more than in any other classical survival the ballerina is purely a virtuoso. Clara is the character and the interest in Clara vanishes after the first act. There is consequently nothing at all for the actress to develop.

Again in her recent interpretation of Swanhilda in *Coppélia* her gift of building a role can be seen to the full. I would draw atten-

[1] Trefilova, greatest of all pure classicists, was a lamentable failure in *Le Spectre de la Rose*. Karsavina remains the most complete of all dancers.

tion in particular to the moment when she pretends to come to life, to the truly moving quality she reveals in a flash. The manner in which she and Coppélius (Helpmann) 'feed' one another results in a sparkling sequence of comedy, adding not merely liveliness but life to the quaintness of an over-familiar work, yet never stepping outside the frame.

Just as in *Casse-Noisette*, and for the same reason, her last act is the least successful. Apart from the total lack of inspiration in the choreography, the drama has finished with the curtain fall and there is no more character to be developed. From a purely period point of view, a perfectly legitimate approach, Fonteyn is not by any means the best Swanhilda I have seen, yet her performance gives me more pleasure than any I can remember save de Valois', in which she had reconciled period and interpretation, and certain moments of Lydia Lopokova's, unforgettable for their spirit of mischief. It is only fair to add that I saw neither in the unsatisfactory last act.

Her work in the modern repertoire has given us a number of creations in varied mood. I would single out as an example a recent role, that of the girl in *The Rake's Progress*. This is pure *demi-caractère* and has been danced with success by Markova, its creator, and by many others. It was danced charmingly by a recruit from the *corps de ballet*. It is appealing and, so to speak, foolproof. Yet Fonteyn gave it an interpretation that made me feel that I was seeing it for the first time. She did not leave the character static, but developed it from the foolish daughter of a mercenary mother to a woman capable of true self-sacrifice. In her make-up, both mental and physical, it was a part of the Hogarth picture, where others had been content to leave it the one pretty element in a coarse picture. That is the very essence of Fonteyn's art: the creation of an initial feeling of completeness, the detail with which that completeness is built up revealing itself performance by performance. It is that, combined with a rare musical quality or, one might say, the result of a rare musical quality, so closely are music and interpretation allied in ballet, that makes her the greatest ballerina among her contemporaries. I must except those Soviet dancers I have not seen and I refuse to make comparisons with the great figures of the past.

The National Ballet may not produce another such ballerina for a considerable time, but it has proved that, given the material, it can bring it to complete artistry.

III. THE MALE DANCER

After the Romantic movement, with its deification of woman, the male dancer disappeared from the scene except as a lifter, a sort of drone, revolving around the Queen Bee. In Russia alone he retained some of his artistic functions and in Russia alone the ballet survived. It is not necessary to stress the importance of the male in the whole artistic balance; you have only to have seen a robust woman Franz in *Coppélia* at the Paris Opéra to realise that, and of all ballets *Coppélia* needs the least male co-operation. Conceive of a *Sylphides* without the male or a female *Spectre de la Rose* to imagine what banality would result. The Russians dazzled Western Europe with *Prince Igor* and the virility of Bolm's dancing attracted more attention than anything else, as the press notices reveal.

The idea of the effeminacy of the male dancer has caused considerable damage. It has arisen from the notoriety of a few unfortunates. It can be stated emphatically that the effeminate dancer is a bad dancer and that the good dancer requires all the attributes of a true athlete. For a long time this was not recognised in England, with the result that often English dancers were of the effeminate type; the wrong kind of boy took up dancing and the fallacy was in danger of becoming a tradition. The first English male dancer to make a name was Anton Dolin. His youth and virtuosity in *The Blue Train* caused a sensation and he followed this up by some fine technical performances in the classics. He has alternated between music-hall and ballet, at times to the detriment of his style. He has been artist and showman, true dancer and the acrobat who invites applause, *danseur noble* and stunt artist. He has always been an outstanding partner. He occupies an important position in the history of English dancing, if not of English ballet. Today, like Markova, he is back in Russian ballet where he truly belongs. The first English dancer to succeed under his own unmistakably English name was Marie Rambert's pupil, Harold Turner. His athletic performances did much to reveal the true function of the male dancer and to banish prejudice. The Camargo Society, the Ballet Club and Sadlers Wells owe him a great deal both directly and indirectly.

But there is another aspect to male dancing than that of athleticism, however important it is to stress that. The classical dancer lifts, he is also the lover and as such must be virile in character as well as physique. In modern ballet the male dancer must be considerably more than a lifter, he must act.

The *premier danseur classique*, opposite number to the ballerina, has a particularly difficult role to fulfil. When he is remembered at all as an individual, he is given a mass of conventional sign-language mime which easily appears ridiculous at the present day. He has got to make it appear spontaneous and convincing. In other words, he has no chance of shining, that is the ballerina's prerogative, but every opportunity of making a complete ass of himself. Lucien Petipa received praise through his very unobtrusiveness! Nijinsky overcame that handicap by lending true conviction to the prince's role in *Giselle* and making of him a character in drama. For the first time critics discovered that this was a role at all. Although the Russian male dancer always had his place, it was Diaghileff who gave him a true status, or rather Fokine, as Harlequin, The Golden Slave, Le Spectre de la Rose; with Massine the list grew. The purely classical male dancer was no longer of supreme importance, the new dancer must be a character actor. Outstanding in this line was Massine. One has only to remember how, from the moment he entered the scene in *Le Beau Danube*, he had established the Hussar's character, and his range extended to the grotesque of the Barman in *Union Pacific* and the Can-Can dancer in *La Boutique Fantasque*. His creations live in the memory of every ballet-lover; they have set a standard for all time.

IV. ROBERT HELPMANN

In Robert Helpmann, an Australian, the National Ballet possesses an equally outstanding personality and perhaps an even more complete actor with a wider range that extends from the dummy in *The Swan Lake* to the drink-sodden manager in *The Prospect Before Us*. Apart from his ability to make one believe in conventional mime, he gives the role a shape. Watch him in the ballroom scene from *The Swan Lake*, when the Queen parades a bevy of court ladies before him and suggests that he choose a wife. It is deliberately restrained, a background as it must be to the dancing, and it is characteristic of Helpmann never to overact or to steal the attention. He is unusually conscientious in carrying out the choreographer's intentions, he never distorts for effect, he fills in the role but never passes beyond its contours. It is another proof of his acting ability that he makes one believe in his own classical dancing. I do not in fact know how good a dancer he is, his technique is so absolutely the servant of his acting. There are probably a score or more male dancers who are far finer classical technicians, yet who produce only half the effect. Once again after Nijinsky he has given meaning to the Prince in *Giselle*.

This leads one to the truism that technique is perfect when it is sufficient for the dancer to express himself through his role completely, that it is imperfect when we are forced to label anyone a 'technical dancer' for lack of a better description. Was Pavlova a great technician? Mechanically many a schoolgirl can exceed her turns without being able to dance. Dancing is rarely learnt in the classroom, it is sometimes forgotten, it is learnt on the stage itself. The majority in most companies never become dancers, they perform rehearsed movements tolerably.

Robert Helpmann is a complete actor in voice as well as in gesture and that is in the great tradition of the past. His early experience in every branch of the theatre and his natural gifts have made him so, but as a dancer he is a product of the method and discipline of the National Ballet. That method has produced the right type of male dancer: Somes, Hart, Carter and others. It is rapidly destroying the prejudice against male dancing. But if the school is to fulfil itself, it must develop an education that will include drama and that will go beyond dance technique.

V. THE COMPANY

I have shown that Sadlers Wells started under a very considerable handicap and I have analysed some of the reasons for its success. I have also talked of the word 'company' as if it were a living individual. A company is made up of a number of individuals who are so trained and disciplined that they have to surrender something of themselves to the common good. The members of the National Ballet have been essentially good citizens of their miniature commonwealth. A remarkable thing has been the loyalty of the men, and, today, the boys. They have stuck to the company when they could have earned far more in some commercial enterprise. Men on leave from the Forces have often spent the whole time dancing. Without such loyalty the Ballet would have been forced to disband and could never have been revived.

The Wells dancers have always believed in the national importance of what they are doing, they have not allowed personal ambition to interfere with their team work. The result has been firstly a remarkable *ensemble*. That has always been a British quality, but there is a difference here. I have watched this company for seasons on end; I know the work of every individual in detail. Visit any ballet for the first time and you will see trim lines, you will not be able to pick out the individuals. Ten years ago these girls would have remained in those lines for the rest of their careers and on the whole, in spite of day-dreams, they would have been content. The English girl's ambition had been largely fulfilled by getting into the ballet at all. Today they are individuals with something of their own to express and they will be given the opportunity. For a ballet or two they may step into the limelight, but that will not damage the *ensemble*. Knowing their work, I am struck more than anything by the latent talent there. Before the National Ballet was formed and in its early days there was little individual talent, while in recent Russian companies every dancer was an individual and there was little *ensemble*.

These dancers by their freedom from jealousy do not necessarily show an angelic disposition, but they do show that they have implicit faith in the integrity of their management.

One of the cardinal rules for the running of any National Ballet with a repertory programme is, apart from the *ballerina* and *premier danseur*, the absence of stars designated as such. The public will make its stars, but in that way it cannot spoil them. One role, two or three dancers, that is the recipe for an all-round company. No management can afford to present its dancers with roles that become their personal property.

The right attitude, the one that our dancers hold today, is that it is an honour not merely to attract attention in such-and-such a role but to be members of the National Ballet.

CHAPTER IX

THE MISSION OF A NATIONAL BALLET

HAD the Ballet merely carried on it would have been an achievement. It has developed and taken shape. Let us try and assess its value, both today and in the future.

In the first place, is ballet a luxury? The fact that Lilian Baylis' audience invariably packed the house at prices ranging from 6d. to 6s. is sufficient answer to that. Entertainment has been recognised as a necessity, even, perhaps especially, at the grimmest moments of war. Moscow has proved that; though the decks were cleared for action ballet was not jettisoned. If entertainment is a necessity, then a type of entertainment that can provide music, décor, drama and dancing is of first value.

What, apart from entertainment, is the special value of a National Ballet? The results achieved by Russia's ballet will answer that question and we in Britain require those results more than any other nation. We have to overcome the absurd notion, which many of us believe, that we are a fundamentally inartistic nation. Through a long connection with the arts in many countries I find that the contrary is the case. Ballet may be the quickest way to cure this national inferiority complex, it is certainly the easiest manner in which to export our art; superficially in a sense, but it can pave the way for concert and art exhibition. The Russian music that we know, the Russian painters and even the literature first came to our attention through her dancers. Ballet is the one universal stage language.

There is another function that I see for a National Ballet. I can only speak here through a close knowledge of one Dominion, but the application is general. Australia before the war was much in the position of this country before the foundation of the Camargo Society. Her audiences were receptive, they had seen and applauded Genée, Pavlova, Spessiva and the young Russians, and were even more critical than ours; it is not so easy to bluff an Australian audience. She was forming dancers of fine physique and of an alert intelligence. The Wells has and has had several other Australian artists besides Helpmann. Given peaceful conditions, it is only a matter of time before the beginning of an all-Australian company. I do not believe that Australian snobbery will prove such a handicap as ours has been, judging by the esteem in which she holds her painters, singers and writers. Then will come the opportunity to exchange companies, artists, choreographers or decorative work, a branch in which the Australians are particularly rich. It will take such a move to convince the British that the Dominions have something artistic of their own to express, worth more than much of the European humbug that they swallow daily. A prominent Australian has only recently told me of the value in national propaganda of the outstanding success of visiting ballet companies to his country. The dancers returned to England and America, full not only of the usual stories of hospitality but with accounts of the rare understanding with which their work had been received. I can see much the same thing in the case of America. It is amazing the little we know of American art. These national bodies can fulfil something quite impossible to the large international travelling ballet. Something more important by far than ballet has ever done or dreamed of doing. This is not mere wishful thinking but the result of an essentially practical knowledge of ballet management and of conditions in the countries involved. This is not the place nor the time to draw up a detailed programme of action, but a scheme that is both economically and artistically sound presents no major difficulties; it is a programme to bear constantly in mind. Well-planned travel, as apart from globe-trotting, not only exports your own creations but enriches your dancers and choreographers.

At the end of the war the company will be faced with various difficult problems. Will it remain in the West End or return to the Wells, or journey between the two? One thing is certain: it will never be able to come back to giving two or three performances a week. Excellent as this is in so many ways, it is economically unsound. For the first time the company has earned the necessary money to branch out. The solution may lie in having two companies, the one for travelling. Whatever happens, a permanent home is essential. It is not for me to attempt to solve these problems, especially without a knowledge of the conditions that will prevail. They must be stated, however.

Next the school; let us hope in its perfected form it takes on under post-war conditions a new significance.

Before the war hundreds, yes *hundreds*, of girls travelled from America, England, the Dominions, with a few from Europe, to study in Paris with the great ballerinas, Kschesinska, Egorova, Presbrajenska and Trefilova. They were then over sixty years of age and their great mission, that of handing over their tradition for safe keeping, has been accomplished. After the war the school of a national ballet that has preserved the classics becomes the only possible academic centre. Already before the war the late André Levinson, a great authority, wrote that the centre of world ballet had shifted to London. The National Ballet School will have to be prepared to cope with those pupils.

It was with many of these things in mind that the Sadlers Wells Ballet Fund was started before the war, to develop educational facilities through acquiring for this country a tradition that could become a heritage, and to insure the dancers so that they could find the security worthy of members of a national ballet. Since the war it has naturally marked time, but it has been able to touch a few of its objects by loans to replace material lost during the invasion of Holland, grants to members of the company in the Forces, and payments to dancers for medical treatment. One day it will become important once again.

Jingoism of any kind is abhorrent, but most especially artistic jingoism. I have always refused to praise any company because it was British, and for many years I was regarded as being bitterly hostile to the enterprise. When it happens to be good and British, that is a very different matter, and the time has come to appreciate it from both points of view, to see its value today, its potential value tomorrow and to do everything to further its success. That does not mean a policy of artistic protection. Competition is health, and if the visitor can show superior art and craft, it is the duty of the critic to point it out and the public to applaud it. Our Ballet was founded on Russian Ballet which in its turn was founded on Italo-French Ballet. If ever we cease to profit by example, we had better close our doors. There is no room for the person who takes sides and who treats an art like an international football match. In our eagerness to pay tribute to our own we must avoid any feeling of smugness. This can only be done by the development of a critical spirit, by a true knowledge of what has happened in the past, and essentially by the realisation that the company is always more important than the individual. It is for this reason that the National Ballet as opposed to the travelling commercial ballet is, taken over the years, eventually the most important creative force.

We have every reason to be satisfied with the beginnings of our own National Ballet and to feel confidence in its future.

Part II

APPENDICES AND NOTES

I. A CRITIC'S PATH

THE writing of this book has necessitated much delving into old press-books and has prompted this brief statement which may be of some interest and value, now that everyone who visits the ballet over once a week is more or less a critic.

I started my criticism with a book, *Some Studies in Ballet*, published seventeen years ago and at my own expense, since there was no vogue then for ballet books. In it I attacked Diaghileff's modernist programme of the *La Chatte* period and took a definite stand for the classics, my thesis being that extreme modernism could lead logically only to the puppet theatre.[1] My education, then very incomplete, had been formed by the works of Fokine, *The Sleeping Princess* (with Trefilova in particular) and by the dancing of Pavlova; I have never committed the sin of using her name by way of comparison. I have re-read that first book, and while there is much in the expression of them to make me smile, I still agree with the general principles laid down. It gained me the friendship of Valerian Svetloff, dean of ballet critics, Vera Trefilova, Fokine, Nijinska, Kschesinska and others. I attended their classes, discussed the tradition of Ballet and of ballets, the interpretation of roles; I even took some classes, and generally learnt my job. In the studios also I saw those six-year-olds who were to be the big names in the ballet of the very near future.

[1] 'It would seem as though the failure of ballet had come from the professed ballet-lovers themselves—those long-haired, effeminate, intellectual snobs who insist upon something new at all costs, something that they alone must be able to understand, or profess to understand. A greater proof of their failure to understand ballet it would be hard to find. The dancers themselves are entirely opposed to the present productions . . . which are appreciated by a very small, noisy clique. The modern "acroballet" is artificially maintained and must die. Whether it will kill ballet or not depends on the time it takes in dying.'—*Some Studies in Ballet*, 1928.

It died very soon afterwards, and ballet survived and flourished.

It may be a mistake for a critic to be familiar with the artists he is to criticise—it certainly creates awkward situations—but in the small world of ballet it cannot possibly be avoided. There is no book to consult as in the drama, the dancer alone has the knowledge and the tradition.

At that time also, under the guidance of Larionov who had performed a similar service for Massine, I visited the various artists' studios and also the scene-painting studios of Allegri and others and learnt something of stage lighting and setting—enough to appreciate its difficulties. If I mention music the last, it is not that I regard it as the least important. I had always been a concert-goer with an average knowledge and a very keen appreciation of Russian and French music.

This theoretical equipment would have been insufficient without some practical knowledge of the working of companies and the economics of ballet. It is so easy to postulate an ideal plan that is impossible of fulfilment, and I have always aimed at being constructive. I travelled many thousands of miles with a number of companies, studying both sides of the house in some detail. As far as a critic could learn so nebulous an art I had learnt ballet. How did I apply my knowledge?

It is difficult to be entirely honest with oneself, but circumstances have made it easier since I can now look back on a closed chapter.

My first phase was that of the enthusiast who wishes to serve, so to speak, as a missionary. I was the critic-propagandist, a dangerous path for the critic, though circumstances at the time justified it. I was successful as a propagandist, but by no means always so successful as a critic. My standards were correct, but I can now see that I indulged in a great deal of wishful thinking, jumped too rapidly to conclusions where I might and should have safeguarded myself and my readers by reserves. I was too honest not to admit that my swan of yesterday was a goose today, which was less than fair to the 'goose' and which created an impression of fickleness and favouritism. The dancers altered, I did not; but of course I was wrong in the first place. It was some time before I realised the problem of the immature dancer and learned patience and moderation.

My most important work in those days lay behind the scenes in a consultative capacity, as an organiser rather than as a critic.

It was the emergence of Sadlers Wells that gave me a jolt and made me reconsider my position. I had first become interested in British Ballet as a possibility through Marie Rambert's brilliant little group. I saw the Wells merely as a background to Markova, which in a sense it was. The hard work and careful planning lay hidden in the rehearsal rooms where I was not welcome. The Wells at that time was touchy and sensitive, even a trifle smug. They did not encourage publicity of any kind, yet felt hurt at not receiving it. Meanwhile my interest was centred on those young dancers I had seen as children at the *barre* in the Paris studios. I had inside knowledge and I revelled in the role of prophet. I was right in many cases, but I can also see how many misses, and not all of them near ones, lie buried in my press-book!

It was when Markova left Sadlers Wells to be replaced by a good all-round company that I realised the important fact that *the company and not the individual is the one thing that matters.* De Basil himself realised this vividly but found it impossible to escape the play of the strong personalities he had created with the help of such enthusiasts as myself during that memorable season of 1933. The Wells was wise in discouraging publicity, for at that period of growth anything that I could have done would have been along the wrong lines. Also the production of new works turned my attention from dancers to choreography. The classical programme fitted in both with my sympathies and early training. Sadlers Wells gave me a closer insight into the workings of Russian Ballet and tempered my enthusiasm. It enabled me, for instance, to appreciate to the full the valuable work of the Philadelphia Ballet, essentially a company, and to make its creations better known.

Certainly I remain an enthusiast, it is impossible to criticise and to be of service to an art without that spur; but today when I have the time I visit the ballet for pleasure and without the need of producing an immediate reaction.

If I have outlined one critic's path, it is not because it is of any particular interest in itself but because so many others are following the same direction. This is a critical moment for the future of an art that can be of inestimable service to the artistic life of this country, and only sober and right thinking can help to bring that about.

Ninette de Valois, *Coppélia*

Frederick Ashton

Pearl Argyle and Robert Helpmann

Alicia Markova, *La Camargo*

Harold Turner, *Carnaval*

Margot Fonteyn and Michael Somes, *Horoscope*

Margot Fonteyn and Robert Helpmann, *Hamlet*

Margot Fonteyn, *The Swan Lake*

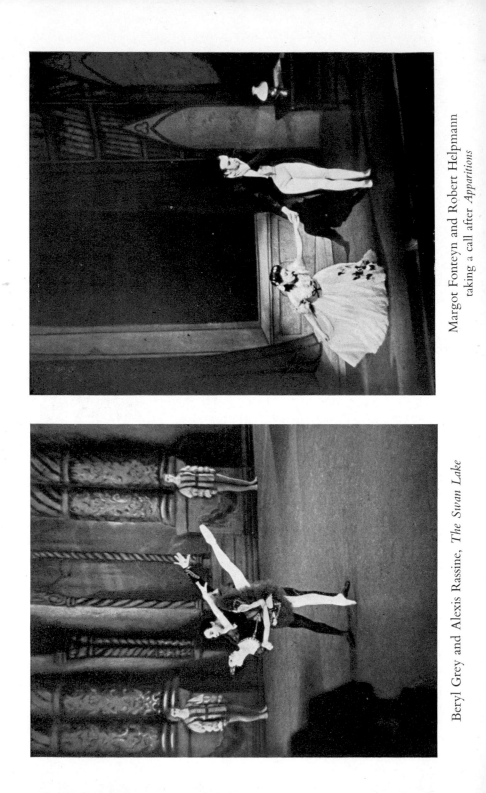

Margot Fonteyn and Robert Helpmann
taking a call after *Apparitions*

Beryl Grey and Alexis Rassine, *The Swan Lake*

June Brae

Pamela May

Margaret Dale and Robert Helpmann
in the Tango from *Façade*

Beryl Grey in *The Swan Lake*
'32 fouettés'

II. BIBLIOGRAPHY OF SADLERS WELLS BALLET

This bibliography shows more clearly than anything the extraordinary rapidity with which the Sadlers Wells Ballet gained recognition. It starts with a few references in books devoted to Russian Ballet, it forms a background to monographs on Markova, then with a rush it comes into its own, taking more and more space in books on the ballet in general, and this, let it be noted, at a time when Russian Ballet was in London for some four months of the year and at the very height of its popularity. Its critics start to praise grudgingly or are frankly disparaging, then in a season or two they accept the company as potentially an equal of the Russians. Other English companies have sprung up but they attract little attention. The critic is interested in continuity and systematic progress.

This bibliography is in itself a recognition of the National Ballet, and some of the books mentioned have gone into many editions. No company has been more fully covered in illustration. While much of this matter rapidly dates and seems trivial today, it will be of value in the future to the historian of our English Ballet, not only for what it says but as a symptom of the enormous popularity gained by Sadlers Wells within a few years of its birth.

1932 HASKELL, Arnold L.
　　　The Ballet in England
　　　52 pp. paper bound
　　　(A reprint of articles from the *New English Weekly*, dealing mainly with the Camargo Season at the Savoy. Of no particular value today, except to the writer as marking a stage in his education.)

1934 STOKES, Adrian
　　　Tonight the Ballet
　　　(Mainly devoted to the de Basil Company. Original and stimulating. Highly critical of English choreography but appreciative of the classics revived at the Wells.)

　　　HASKELL, Arnold L.
　　　Balletomania
　　　(Chapter X, 'English Interlude'. The references to Sadlers Wells

and English choreography seem grudging[1] but in view of the date were not unjust and set the new company a high standard.)

1935 BENTLEY, Nicholas
Ballet-Hoo
(A delightful reaction from such books as *Balletomania*, containing much sound criticism, though a trifle grudging in its references to the English effort.)

ANTHONY, Gordon
Alicia Markova
(Camera studies of Markova at Sadlers Wells.)

BEAUMONT, Cyril
Alicia Markova
(An illustrated monograph dealing largely with Markova at Sadlers Wells. 25 pp. 12 plates.)

BEAUMONT, Cyril
The Vic-Wells Ballet
(An illustrated monograph. 25 pp. 12 plates.)

(No date) HOWLETT, Jasper
Talking of Ballet
(Discussed from the point of view of a well-informed member of the audience. Goes up to the creation of *The Rake's Progress*. 138 pp. 8 photographs.)

1936 BRAHMS, Caryl (editor)
Footnotes to the Ballet
(A book of essays by various authors including Constant Lambert. Sadlers Wells referred to on pp. viii, xvi, xviii, 22, 26, 27, 46, 50, 123-6, 261-2. And plates on pp. 60, 121, 157, 241, 248, 249.)

HASKELL, Arnold L.
Prelude to Ballet
(Sadlers Wells, pp. 72-5, 105, 106. Contains the footnote 'Perhaps some day Fonteyn will bring *Giselle* back to life again. There are many signs to suggest this possibility.' Portrait of Fonteyn on wrapper of half the edition.)

HEPPENSTALL, Rayner
An Apology for Dancing
(Involved and totally beyond my comprehension.)

[1] 'It has yet to prove itself by creating its own *ballerina*. So far it is an encouraging local phenomenon, a plucky prelude to bigger things. . . . The Vic-Wells has vast opportunities, and it would be an unfriendly act to damn it with faint praise, or even just to be grateful for what it gives. It can do so much better, and I like to believe it will.'

1937 DE VALOIS, Ninette
    Invitation to the Ballet
(This important book does not deal exclusively with the Vic-
Wells; on the contrary it is a plea for an objective view of ballet.
304 pp. 40 illustrations.)

HASKELL, Arnold L.
    Dancing Round the World
(Part II is a study of contemporary ballet in general and shows the
benefits acquired by the sound planning of the Wells, the progress made in all directions and the dangers of the disunity in the
many Russian companies. Many illustrations.)

BEAUMONT, Cyril
    Complete Book of Ballets
(An invaluable book of reference, and like everything done by
this author, meticulous and detailed. Includes works by de Valois,
pp. 927-39, and Ashton, pp. 988-97, also illustrations.)

BEAUMONT, Cyril
    Design for the Ballet
(A very important collection and the only one of its kind. Includes décor for *Nocturne, Wedding Bouquet, Les Patineurs, Le Lac
des Cygnes, The Rake's Progress, Casse-Noisette, Le Baiser de la Fée,
Apparitions, Giselle, The Gods Go A-Begging, The Haunted Ballroom, The Jar, My Lord of Burleigh*.)

ANTHONY, Gordon
    Ballet
(Camera studies, with an introduction and notes by Arnold L.
Haskell. 32 plates devoted to the Vic-Wells Ballet.)

1938 COTON, A. V.
    A Prejudice for Ballet
('A Prejudice' expressed in a manner that I do not understand,
but well illustrated.)

HARCOURT-WILLIAMS (editor)
    Vic-Wells: The Work of Lilian Baylis
(A memorial volume, having articles by Ninette de Valois,
Robert Helpmann, and some illustrations of the Ballet.)

SEVERN, Merlyn
    Ballet in Action
(With an introductory essay and critical notes by Arnold L.
Haskell. Brilliant action photographs of *Checkmate, Wedding
Bouquet, Apparitions, Les Rendezvous, Le Baiser de la Fée*.)

ANTHONY, Gordon
The Vic-Wells Ballet
(Camera studies and an important 24-pp. introduction by Ninette de Valois. 55 full-page illustrations.)

HASKELL, Arnold L.
Ballet Panorama. An illustrated chronicle of three centuries. (Sadlers Wells situated in the history of ballet; references and 22 plates and Beaton's décor for *Apparitions* in colour. New edition, 1943, has additional material on Sadlers Wells in war-time.)

HASKELL, Arnold L.
Ballet. A complete guide to appreciation.
(Pelican Special.)
(Dedicated to Ninette de Valois and contains a long study of her work and personality. References to Sadlers Wells on pp. 44, 68, 72, 91, 129, 130 *et seq.*, 140, 141, 178-86, 201-7 and illustrations.)

HASKELL, Arnold L.
Felicity Dances
(Fiction: A children's tale about the Ballet; some of the episodes concern Sadlers Wells.)

DOLIN, Anton
Ballet-go-round
(Autobiography of Dolin, containing fleeting references to his appearances at Sadlers Wells, etc.)

1939 HASKELL, Arnold L.
Birth of the English Ballet
(Journal of Royal Society of Arts, June 16th, 1939. Paper won the Society's silver medal. 7 photographs. Introduction by Ninette de Valois.)

HASKELL, Arnold L.
Balletomane's Album
(Introduction and 152 illustrations, 55 devoted to Sadlers Wells. Fonteyn on wrapper; end-paper with facsimile autographs of company.

1940 (actually published 1942) ANTHONY, Gordon
The Sleeping Princess
(Camera studies with the following articles: Tchaikovsky and the Ballet, by Constant Lambert (12 pp.); Décor and Costumes, by Nadia Benois (5 pp.); 'Aurora Truly Wedded', by Arnold L. Haskell (12 pp.); and appendix of casts in various productions. 63 plates.)

HASKELL, Arnold L. (editor)
Ballet to Poland
(A collection of essays and photographs, among which articles by
de Valois and Lambert. Frontispiece, McKnight Kauffer's design
for the Black Queen in *Checkmate*; numerous photographs including a series of *Dante Sonata*.)

1941 ANTHONY, Gordon
Margot Fonteyn
(23 camera studies and 5 pp. appreciation by Eveleigh Leith.)

1942 ANTHONY, Gordon
The Sadler Wells Ballet
(47 camera studies. 8 pp. introduction by Eveleigh Leith.)

AMBROSE, Kay
Balletomane's Sketch-Book
(220 drawings, 80 photographs. Introduced by Arnold L. Haskell.
Sadlers Wells, Section V, pp. 37-67.)

BEAUMONT, Cyril
Supplement to Complete Book of Ballets
Ashton, pp. 113-14, de Valois, 67-71.

MANCHESTER, P. W.
Vic-Wells: A Ballet Progress
(An interesting study of the company as it strikes a critically
minded member of the audience. Illustrations.)

1943 AMBROSE, Kay
Ballet Lovers' Pocket Book
64 pp.
(No direct mention of Sadlers Wells but drawings clearly taken
from Wells' artists.)

I have not listed articles and magazines. Readers are
referred to the *Dancing Times* for the whole of the
period and to *The Bystander* for a fine photographic
record.

III. KEY DATES IN THE CREATION OF A NATIONAL BALLET, WITH COMMENTARY

I HAVE not wished to burden the text with dates or to give a purely factual account of the birth and progress of British Ballet, but since this is the only record of the movement from its beginnings, I have thought it important to include a chronology of thirty years which complements the text. Non-British events of great influence are placed in brackets.

1910 (First appearance in London of Anna Pavlova.)
      First number of the *Dancing Times*. This monthly has through the personality of its editor, P. J. S. Richardson, played a very important role in founding our Ballet. It has taken the lead in every movement, has been the mouthpiece of all our aspirations. It would be possible to write a large volume on the positive work it has achieved. This is a good year in which to start our record.

1911 (The first Diaghileff season.)

1912 Hilda Munnings joins the Diaghileff Ballet as Lydia Sokolova.

1913 Phyllis Bedells *première danseuse* at the Empire.
      She succeeded Lydia Kyasht.

1914 Astafieva starts her London school.

1917 (Genée's farewell at the Coliseum.)
      I mention this farewell because, starting with the year 1910, I have not been able to give Genée the prominence she deserves in the popularisation of dancing as an art. With her retirement as a dancer begins her active interest in the dancing profession in England.

1919 Ninette de Valois *première danseuse* at Royal Opera, Covent Garden.

1920 Foundation of Association of Operatic Dancing of Great Britain under the presidency of Adeline Genée and the secretaryship of P. J. S. Richardson.

1921 (*The Sleeping Princess*. Alhambra.)

1922 Foundation of the Cecchetti Society.
      This effort to codify and preserve the maestro's teaching in England was all-important; its committee included Marie Rambert, Ninette de Valois and Cyril Beaumont.

78

1923 Astafieva presents a pupil show, 'Anglo-Russian Ballet', at the Coliseum.
First appearance of Patrick Kay as Anton Dolin, and success of a child, Alice Marks, later Markova. De Valois joins the Diaghileff Ballet.

1924 Anton Dolin joins the Diaghileff Ballet.

1925 Alicia Markova joins the Diaghileff Ballet.

1926 Ashton's first ballet—*The Tragedy of Fashion*.
De Valois opens Academy of Choreographic Art.

1928 H.M. the Queen becomes a patron of the Association of Operatic Dancing.
Ninette de Valois produces *Rout*.

1929 (Death of Diaghileff.)
P. J. S. Richardson and Arnold Haskell organise a series of dinners to which leading members of the profession are invited to arrange for the foundation of a Ballet Producing Society.

1930 Inaugural dinner of the Camargo Society.
Marie Rambert's dancers appear at the Lyric, Hammersmith, in productions by Frederick Ashton and Susan Salaman. This first positive sign of creation is an all-important landmark. Harold Turner, one of Marie Rambert's group, dances *Le Spectre de la Rose* with Karsavina at the Arts Theatre.
The Camargo Society produces *Pomona* (October 19th).
Harold Turner and Frederick Ashton appear at the Arts Theatre with Lopokova and dance in creations by Ashton.
André Levinson writing of this year in *Comoedia* noted that London was becoming the ballet centre of the world.

1931 (Death of Anna Pavlova.)
Foundation by Marie Rambert and Ashley Dukes of the Ballet Club (see p. 16).
Formation of a permanent company under Ninette de Valois at Sadlers Wells.
Production by the Camargo Society of *Job*, *Façade*, *Rio Grande*, etc.

1932 Productions at the Camargo Society, the Vic-Wells and the Ballet Club. Markova appears in all three. Camargo Society's season at the Savoy with Spessiva and Lopokova as guest artists.

1933 Robert Helpmann joins Sadlers Wells.
Coppélia added to Wells repertoire.
(*Les Ballets 1933* with Toumanova, Tilly Losch, Pearl Argyle, Diana Gould.)
(De Basil's record season at the Alhambra.)

1934 *Casse-Noisette* added to Wells repertoire.
      Lac des Cygnes in full added to Wells repertoire.
      Death of Astafieva.

1935 Creation of *The Rake's Progress.*
      Margot Fonteyn's first lead in revival of *Rio Grande.*
      Alicia Markova leaves the Wells. Formation of Markova–Dolin Ballet.
      Phyllis Bedells' farewell matinée.

1936 Tudor's *Jardin aux Lilas* at Ballet Club.
      Ashton's *Apparitions, Nocturne* at Wells.
      Arnold Haskell founds the Vic–Wells Ballet Fund.
      Margot Fonteyn guest at the Ballet Club. This shows a continued close collaboration between the creative elements in British ballet.

1937 Margot Fonteyn dances *Giselle* at Sadlers Wells.
      Ashton's *Les Patineurs* and *Wedding Bouquet.*
      The Wells visits Paris and de Valois' *Checkmate* has its première.
      University Extension Lectures (London) on the *History, Meaning and Influence of the Dance.*
      Death of Lilian Baylis.
      (A significant year in which de Basil, Blum and the Wells play simultaneously and practically to capacity. Other visitors to London are the Philadelphia Ballet, Uday Shankar, the Polish Ballet.)

1938 Ashton's *Horoscope* at Sadlers Wells.
      H.M. the Queen present at Gala Performance in aid of the Vic–Wells Ballet Fund.

1939 Revival of *The Sleeping Princess* in its entirety and its performance at the Covent Garden Gala in honour of President Lebrun.[1]

1940 Sadlers Wells tour of Holland, resulting in loss of material and narrow escape of the company.
      Production of Ashton's *Wanderer, Dante Sonata, Wise and Foolish Virgins.*
      September, the Wells closed. Company tours with 2 pianos.

1941 Bronson Albery becomes a Governor of the Vic–Wells and the company is given its big chance by a new H.Q. at the New Theatre.
      Helpmann's first ballet, *Comus.*

1942 Helpmann's *Hamlet* and *The Birds.*

1943 Ashton's *The Quest.*

[1] It is interesting to note that the following scheme was interrupted by the outbreak of war: (1) Enlargement of the School. (2) Education at Sadlers Wells. (3) Formation of a 2nd company. (4) Employment of a distinguished guest choreographer for a 2-year period. (5) One work a year as an experiment by a young choreographer of the English school. This would have been begun by the end of 1939.

IV. THE CHOREOGRAPHY OF FREDERICK ASHTON

Year	Ballet	Author	Composer	Décors and Costumes	Original Cast	Created for
1926	Tragedy of Fashion	Ashley Dukes	E. Goossens	S. Fedorovitch	Rambert, F. James, F. Ashton	Presented by Marie Rambert and later in *Riverside Nights*, Lyric, Hammersmith
1930	Capriol Suite	Ashton	P. Warlock	W. Chappell	Argyle, Howard, Hyman, Gould, Chappell, Turner, Ashton	Marie Rambert. At Lyric, Hammersmith, and later the Ballet Club
1930	Florentine Picture	Ashton	Corelli	After Italian Masters	Rambert and Company	Marie Rambert
1930	Leda	Ashton	Gluck	Chappell	Gould, Ashton	Marie Rambert
1931	Foyer de la Danse	Ashton	Berners	After Degas	Ashton, Markova	Marie Rambert
1931	La Péri	Dukas	Dukas	Chappell	Markova, Ashton	Marie Rambert
1931	Lady of Shalott	After Tennyson	Sibelius	Chappell	Argyle, Ashton	Marie Rambert
1931	Mars and Venus	Ashley Dukes	Scarlatti	..	Argyle, Turner	For Lang's *Jew Süss*, afterwards at Ballet Club, amplified
1931	Mephisto Valse	Lenan	Liszt	Feodorovitch	Markova, Gore, Ashton	Marie Rambert
1931	Mercure	Ashton	Satie	Chappell	Karsavina, Ashton, Chappell	Marie Rambert, Lyric, Hammersmith
1933	Les Masques	Ashton	Poulenc	Fedorovitch	Markova, Argyle, Gore, Ashton	Marie Rambert
1935	Les Petits Riens	Ashton	Mozart	Chappell	Rambert, Argyle, Turner, Ashton	Marie Rambert

The Choreography of Frederick Ashton (contd.)

Year	Ballet	Author	Composer	Décors and Costumes	Original Cast	Created for
1935	Valentine's Eve	Ashton	Ravel	Fedorovitch	Ashton, Argyle	Marie Rambert (Duke of York's Season)
*1930	The Tartans*	Ashton*	Boyce*	Chappell*	Lopokova, Ashton, Turner	For Lopokova season Arts Theatre
1930	Passionate Pavane	Ashton	Dowland	Chappell	Lopokova, Ashton, Turner	For Lopokova season Arts Theatre
*1931	The First Shoot*	O. Sitwell*	W. Walton*	C. Beaton	Clare Luce and Ashton	For C. B. Cochran Revue
1932	Récamier	Ashton	Schubert	Chappell	Argyle and Ashton	For C. B. Cochran at Trocadero
*1930	Pomona*	Lambert* Ashton	Lambert*	Banting*	Ludmilla and Dolin	For Camargo Society
1931	Façade		Walton	Armstrong	Lopokova, Markova, Ashton	For Camargo Society
1931	My Lord of Burleigh	E. Evans	Mendelssohn	Sheringham revival Derek Hill	Markova, Argyle, Gould, Hyman, Chappell	For Camargo Society
1931	Rio Grande	Lambert	Lambert	Burra	Lopokova, Markova, Gore, Chappell	For Camargo Society
1932	High Yellow (with B. Bradley)	..	Spike Hughes	V. Bell	Markova, Sonne, Ashton	For Camargo Society
1933	Les Rendezvous	Ashton	Auber (arr. Lambert)	Chappell	Markova, Argyle, Gould, Hyman, Chappell	For Camargo Society
1933	Regatta	Ashton	Gavin Gordon	Chappell	De Valois, Judson, Chappell	For Camargo Society
*1934	4 Saints in 3 Acts*	G. Stein*	V. Thompson*	F. Stetheimer*	All Negro	44th St. Theatre, N.Y.

Year	Ballet	Author	Composer	Décors and Costumes	Original Cast	Created for
1935	Le Baiser de la Fée	Stravinsky	Stravinsky	Fedorovitch	Fonteyn, Argyle, Turner	Sadlers Wells
1936	Apparitions	Lambert	Liszt (selected Lambert; orchestrated Jacob)	Beaton	Fonteyn, Somes, Helpmann	Sadlers Wells
1936	Nocturne	E. Sackville West	Delius ('Paris')	Fedorovitch	Fonteyn, Brae, Ashton, Helpmann	Sadlers Wells
1937	Les Patineurs	Ashton	Meyerbeer (arr. Lambert)	Chappell	Honer, Miller, Fonteyn, Turner, Helpmann	Sadlers Wells
1937	Siesta	Ashton	Walton	Fedorovitch	Argyle, Helpmann	Sadlers Wells
1937	Wedding Bouquet	Berners and Stein	Berners	Berners	Fonteyn, Brae, Farron, Helpmann	Sadlers Wells
1938	The Devil's Holiday		Paganini	Berman	Danilova, Franklin	Massine Co. at Monte Carlo
1938	Harlequin in the Street	Ashton	Couperin (orch. Jacob)	Derain	Brae, Carter	Sadlers Wells
1938	Horoscope	Lambert	Lambert	Fedorovitch	Fonteyn, May, Somes	Sadlers Wells
1938	Judgement of Paris	Ashton	L. Berkeley	Chappell	Argyle, Helpmann	Sadlers Wells
1939	Cupid and Psyche	Berners	Berners	Francis Rose	Farron and Staff	Sadlers Wells
1940	Dante Sonata	Ashton	Liszt	Fedorovitch after Flaxman	Fonteyn, Brae, Somes, Helpmann	Sadlers Wells
1940	The Wanderer	Ashton	Schumann	Sutherland	Fonteyn, May, Helpmann, Somes	Sadlers Wells
1940	Wise and Foolish Virgins	From the parable	Bach (arranged Walton)	Rex Whistler	Fonteyn, Honer, Somes	Sadlers Wells
1943	The Quest	Doris Langley Moore	Walton	Piper	Fonteyn, Helpmann, Grey, Franca	Sadlers Wells

V. A NOTE ON THE CLASSICS IN THE WELLS REPERTOIRE

Giselle

2-act ballet by V. de St. Georges, Théophile Gautier and Coralli—music by A. Adam—choreography Coralli. First produced in 1841 and since then continuously. Original cast: Carlotta Grisi as Giselle and Lucien Petipa as Albrecht. In our times Giselle has been interpreted by Pavlova, Karsavina, Spessivtseva, Nemchinova (a different version), Semenova, Markova (its first English interpreter), Toumanova and Fonteyn. Albrecht by Vladimiroff, Novikoff, Nijinsky, Dolin, Lifar, Obouhoff and Helpmann. Revived at Sadlers Wells for Alicia Markova with décor and costumes by William Chappell.

Coppélia

Ballet in 2 acts and 3 scenes by C. Nuittier and A. Saint-Léon. Music, L. Delibes. Choreography, L. Mérante. First produced at the Paris Opéra 1870. The original Swanhilda was Mlle Bozacchi. Its creator, who died shortly afterwards, was only fifteen years old. *Coppélia* was first seen in England with Genée in 1906. Revived at Sadlers Wells with Lydia Lopokova 1933, and later with de Valois, Elizabeth Miller, Mary Honer, Peggy Van Praagh and Margot Fonteyn. Was also revived in a slightly different version by René Blum for Nemchinova and in Massine's company for Danilova.

Le Lac des Cygnes

Ballet in 4 acts. Music by Tchaikovsky. Choreography by Petipa and Ivanoff. First produced at the Maryinsky Theatre in 1895 after a first failure with a different production in 1877. Original cast, Legnani as Odette and Odile. The role has been associated with Kschesinska, the first Russian ballerina to master the now simple 32 *fouettés*, Pavlova, Karsavina, Trefilova, Preobrajenska who came to London with it in 1912, Spessivtseva, Nemchinova, Markova and Fonteyn. In its abbreviated form by Danilova, Baronova, Toumanova, Gollner. Revived by Diaghileff in a 2-act version in 1924 for Trefilova, in 1925 as a divertissement *Le Bal du Lac des Cygnes* for Markova in Monte Carlo and in 1926 in the popular 1-act version. Revived by Sadlers Wells in full for Markova 1934. Décors and costumes by Hugh Stevenson. 1943 new décors and costumes by Leslie Hurry. The most popular Soviet ballet today with the ballerina Ulanova and others.

The Sleeping Princess

Ballet in 5 scenes by Petipa. Music Tchaikovsky, choreography Petipa. First produced at the Maryinsky in 1890. Aurora, Carlotta Brianza. Revived by Diaghileff with additions and alterations by Nijinska and settings by Bakst, Alhambra 1921. Aurora: Trefilova (and

*"Quite honestly I don't know who they are—but they always appear when
we have swans on the lake"*

Spessivtseva and Egorova). Lilac Fairy: Lopokova. Blue Bird: Idzikov-
ski and Lopokova. Revived later as a divertissement *Aurora's Wedding*
by Diaghileff and de Basil. Revived in full at Sadlers Wells 1939 with
Margot Fonteyn as Aurora. Décor and costumes by Nadia Benois
(see Gordon Anthony's album).

Casse-Noisette
    Ballet in 2 acts and 3 scenes by I. Ivanoff. Music by Tchaikovsky;
choreography by Ivanoff. First produced Maryinsky Theatre 1892 with
Dell' Era as the Sugar Plum Fairy. Revived by the René Blum Com-
pany in a modernised version. Revived by Sadlers Wells 1934 with
Markova as the Sugar Plum Fairy. Has since been danced by Argyle,
Honer and Margot Fonteyn.

VI. THE COMPANY IN 1931, 1935 AND 1943

Original Vic-Wells Company, May 5th, 1931

Beatrice Appleyard — Frieda Bamford — Hedley Briggs — Anne Coventry—Stanley Judson—Sheila McCarthy—Ursula Moreton—Marie Neilson—Nadina Newhouse—Claude Newman—Joy Newton.

Conductor: Constant Lambert.
Director: Ninette de Valois.
Ballet Mistress: Ursula Moreton.
Stage Manager: Henry Robinson.

Vic-Wells Company in 1935

At the time of Markova's departure leading members of the company were: Pearl Argyle—June Brae—Alan Carter—William Chappell—Margot Fonteyn—Robert Helpmann—Mary Honer—Pamela May—Elizabeth Miller—Claude Newman—Michael Somes—Harold Turner.

Vic-Wells Company in 1943 (in alphabetical order)

Jean Bedells—Anthony Burke—Pauline Clayden—Margaret Dale—Nigel Desmond—Pauline Dunning—Leslie Edwardes—Joyce Farron—John Field—Margot Fonteyn—Celia Franca—Moyra Fraser—Patricia Garnett—Beryl Grey—Gordon Hamilton—Robert Helpmann—Wenda Horsburgh—Mavis Jackson—Margaret Kelly—Elizabeth Kennedy—Anne Lascelles—Mary Loraine—Lorna Mossford—Joy Newton—Palma Nye—David Paltenghi—Guinevere Parry—Ray Powell—Alexis Rassine—Moira Shearer—Joan Sheldon—Peggy Van Praagh—June Vincent—Franklin White.

Director: Ninette de Valois.
Ballet Mistress: Joy Newton.
Academic Tuition: Peggy Van Praagh.
Musical Director: Constant Lambert.
Conductors: C. Lambert and Julian Clifford.
Stage Director: Henry Arneil.
Stage Manager: Henry Robinson.

VII. NOTES ON THE MUSIC OF THE WELLS PRODUCTIONS

WORKS BY CONSTANT LAMBERT

(i) ORIGINAL

Pomona. Written in 1926. First produced by Nijinska in Buenos Aires 1927. Produced by Camargo Society 1930. Taken over by Sadlers Wells.

Rio Grande. Written in 1927 as a choral work on a poem by Sacheverell Sitwell. Concert version 1930. Produced as a ballet by Camargo Society. Taken over by Sadlers Wells.

Horoscope. Music and book by Constant Lambert. Written for Sadlers Wells. Lost during tour of Holland 1940.

(ii) ARRANGEMENTS

Apparitions. Book by Constant Lambert. Music by Liszt (mostly from posthumous and unknown piano works). Arranged by Lambert and orchestrated by Gordon Jacob.

Les Patineurs. Music by Meyerbeer, arranged by Lambert from *Le Prophète* and *L'Étoile du Nord.*

Les Rendezvous. Music by Auber, arranged by Lambert from *L'Enfant Prodigue.*

Comus. Music by Purcell, arranged by Lambert from various theatrical works and slightly rescored by Lambert.

The Prospect Before Us. Book by Ninette de Valois. Music arranged by Lambert and slightly rescored from instrumental works of William Boyce (1710–79).

Dante Sonata. Music by Liszt (Fantasia quasi sonata—Après une lecture de Dante). Orchestrated by Lambert. First version lost in Holland. Rescored for smaller orchestra. (Pianoforte and orchestra.)

The Wise Virgins. Music by Bach, arranged by Lambert from the religious cantatas, orchestrated by William Walton.

Harlequin in the Street. Music by Couperin, arranged by Lambert, orchestrated by Gordon Jacob. Book by Lambert and Ashton but attributed by them to a contemporary of Couperin.

Prometheus. Book by Lambert. Music by Beethoven, arranged by Lambert. 1936.

Orpheus and Eurydice. Music by Gluck. Slight arrangement by Lambert. 1942.

Fête Polonaise. Music by Glinka, arranged by Lambert.

THE MUSIC OF OTHER WELLS PRODUCTIONS

(a) BY ENGLISH COMPOSERS

Berners. *Wedding Bouquet*. For Sadlers Wells.
   Cupid and Psyche. ,,   ,,   ,,

Bradford. *Jackdaw and the Pigeons*. 1931. (First performed at the 'Vic' at the first performance by the new company, choreography by de Valois, décor W. Chappell. Later produced by the Camargo Society.)

Bliss. *Checkmate*. (Produced by arrangement with the British Council and first performed in Paris.)

Delius. *Nocturne*. (Ballet made on the composer's 'Paris'.)

Gavin Gordon. *Regatta*. 1932.
     Scorpions of Ysit. 1932.
     The Rake's Progress. 1935.

Toye. *Douanes*.
  The Haunted Ballroom.

Vaughan Williams. *Job*.

William Walton. *Façade* (Written originally for recitation of poem by Edith Sitwell.)
     Siesta. (A divertissement for two dancers.)
     The Quest. (Composed for Sadlers Wells.)

(b) BY FOREIGN COMPOSERS

Casella. *The Jar*. Wells ballet by de Valois. (Originally produced by Swedish Ballet, choreography J. Borlin, décors by Chirico.)

Chopin. *Les Sylphides*. Wells version orchestrated by Gordon Jacob.

Françaix. *Le Roi Nu*. Wells ballet by de Valois. (Originally produced at Paris Opéra by Lifar.)

Handel. *The Gods Go A-Begging*. Arranged by Sir Thomas Beecham for Diaghileff.

Mendelssohn. *My Lord of Burleigh*. Arranged by Edwin Evans, orchestrated by Gordon Jacob.

Milhaud. *La Création du Monde*. Ballet by de Valois. (Originally by J. Borlin, Swedish Ballet.) 1923.

Respighi. *The Birds*. Based on old masters. (Originally produced as a ballet in Rome.) Book by Lambert.

Rieti. *Barabau*. Choral ballet by de Valois. (Originally commissioned by Diaghileff.)

Schumann.   *Carnaval*. Wells version orchestrated by Gordon Jacob.

The Wanderer. First produced with 2 pianos. Liszt's arrangement for piano and orchestra now used.

Stravinsky.   *Le Baiser de la Fée*. Based on material from Tchaikovsky. (Originally commissioned by Ida Rubinstein.)

Tchaikovsky.   *The Swan Lake.*

The Sleeping Princess.

Casse-Noisette.

Hamlet. (Original ballet by Helpmann, see p. 52.) Overture—fantaisie and not the later composed incidental music.

VIII. THE YEARLY REPERTOIRE FROM 1935

1935–6 *The Haunted Ballroom—Façade—Casse-Noisette*, Act II—*Les Sylphides—Douanes—Coppélia—The Rake's Progress—Job—Rio Grande—Blue Bird* (pas de deux)—*Les Rendezvous—The Swan Lake—Carnaval—The Sleeping Princess* (pas de deux). NEW BALLETS: *Le Baiser de la Fée—The Gods Go A-Begging—Siesta—Apparitions—Barabau.*

1936–7 Add *Prometheus—Nocturne—Casse-Noisette* (in full)—*Giselle—Les Patineurs—Wedding Bouquet.*

1937–8 Add *Pomona—Checkmate—My Lord of Burleigh—Horoscope—Le Roi Nu—The Swan Lake* (in full).

1938–9 Add *Harlequin in the Street—The Sleeping Princess—Cupid and Psyche.*

War season at the Wells, Jan. 1939–40. Repertoire included *The Sleeping Princess—Checkmate—Les Patineurs—Les Rendezvous—Giselle—Horoscope—Carnaval—The Swan Lake*, Act II—*Façade—Apparitinos—Les Sylphides—Harlequin in the Street—The Rake's Progress* and *Dante Sonata.*

April 1940. Add *The Swan Lake—Job—Nocturne—Coppélia—The Wise Virgins.*

June–Sept. Add *The Prospect Before Us.*

INDEX

THE END

Printed in Great Britain by R. & R. CLARK, LIMITED, Edinburgh.